The Fire of Truth

Vincent C. Talley

The Fire of Truth

Vincent C. Talley

SBPC

Simms Books Publishing Corporation

SBPC

SIMMS BOOKS PUBLISHING CORP.

Publishers Since 2012

Published By Simms Books Publishing

Jonesboro, GA

2********

Library of Congress Cataloging in Publication Data

Vincent C. Talley

The Fire of Truth

ISBN: 978-1-949433-66-1

Printed in the United States of America

Book Arrangement by Simms Books Publishing

Dedication

This book is dedicated to the United States of America, to the dangerous times we are living in, and to the Patriots who are willing to speak out, to stand in the fire of truth, and to take whatever comes. I pray that our country, as we know it, can truly be saved and remain free for future generations. If it is, it will undoubtedly be because of you.

America was not created with cowardice, and it cannot remain with it. Courage, resolve, and love are what is needed to defend us.

Table of Contents

Chapter 1: Unbridgeable

It is said that if you want to help yourself, tell others what they want to hear. But if you want to help people, tell them the truth. Some of the things I write may seem inappropriate, mean-spirited, even cruel—but it comes from a place of love.

We can all agree that most Americans love our country. It may be at different levels, and we may feel more strongly about some things than others, but at the end of the day, we could always agree to disagree. Those of us who pay attention can see this changing more and more before our very eyes.

Most people used to be able to disagree with anyone and still think they were just good people with bad ideas. Now, many of us look at them as bad people with evil ideas. I've always tried to see both sides of any argument, and I'm not afraid to change my mind if the other side simply makes more sense. I've always believed people could think clearly and logically if they just used facts, common sense, and not emotion.

Unfortunately, that's no longer the case. Objective truth, logical thinking, and rational thought have become far less important and have taken a backseat to emotion, political correctness, racial issues, and more. God-given, battle-tested common sense, faith, and decency are no longer our North Star. Many now believe that "north" is whatever they think or feel it is. Because of this, they are unwilling—or unable—to see objective truth. If north is whatever I say it is, then there is no north.

We are living in the age of "My Truth," which technically means a person's subjective experience, belief, or opinion about a situation or event. It basically means, "This is my opinion. The truth is whatever I feel or say it is—and you need to accept it or suffer the consequences." This threat can translate into a variety of actions: being called derogatory names, being banned on Facebook or Twitter (before the name change), or demands to boycott sponsors of national and local news shows to get their hosts suspended.

Many conservative hosts, along with other well-known people, have been threatened, assaulted, even physically attacked in restaurants and other public places. They must have security at speaking events and at their homes due to threats of intimidation and violence. This type of outrageous behavior is almost never seen being perpetrated on liberal Democrats.

Surprisingly, to those not paying attention, some government institutions, school districts, and businesses have bent to this altar of cowardice. Because young boys and men feel and believe they are female, they are allowed to walk around women's locker rooms naked and participate in their sporting events. They have proudly won competitions and awards in weightlifting, track, swimming, and others.

Of course, most officials in charge have been shamed into silence. So have many of the female athletes—even though they are the victims in all of this. These athletes are afraid of what consequences may come from their school officials if they speak out or boycott these events. Most parents themselves have been strangely quiet. I cannot help but ask: Where is the outrage? Where is the shame from everyone involved in this travesty?

Years ago, if you had brought this up at a gathering at your office or home, you would have been laughed out of the room. If President Trump or another well-known conservative had come to these colleges to speak, there would have been outrage—students walking out of classes to protest. They would need security to calm everything down. But for this nonsense? Crickets. The silence is deafening.

Did this happen to society overnight? Or is it more like the frog in a pot of water, slowly heating until it boils? This is what happens when objective truth can be questioned simply because we don't want to hurt anyone's feelings.

If your kids can make decisions about being a boy or girl—and whether or not they need to lose body parts—why not just give them the keys to your car if they're that mature? Let them decide how much candy they can eat, or whether they should take orders from you at all. At what point in this liberal nonsense do people who support it stand up and say, "Enough"?

The sad answer is: if you're waiting for these people to come to their senses, get comfortable—and hopefully you brought your blanket and toothbrush. I wish I could say this was the worst-case scenario. Unfortunately, it's not.

There are transgender women (really men) being sent to women's prisons because of these ridiculous policies. The results are what you'd expect: anger, confusion, and everyone with common sense wondering, "What the hell are these people thinking?" Transgender women assaulting female inmates, reports of rape, lawsuits trying to avoid being sent to men's prisons—none of this should surprise anyone.

Entertaining this nonsense would sound ridiculous to any logically thinking person—but not to the liberal Democrat mindset. Ironically, I think you'd have to be highly educated—with a college degree, master's, or PhD—to be this stupid. Better ideas and opinions would probably come from the guy who does your lawn work or your local plumber.

It's just one more reason that when most of us logical thinkers hear comments from so-called experts, we're skeptical. And we have good reason to be. There are endless examples of policies, issues, and emotional nonsense where the news trots out an "expert" to convince us it all makes sense. Their opinions and predictions are often just educated guesses—and many times, flat-out wrong.

These are just some of the reasons many of us are no longer impressed by college degrees and credentials. It's like a highly educated person telling you about their intellectual achievements, then trying to explain why looking both ways before crossing the street is a dumb idea. It discounts everything they've said.

Even more frustrating, most Democrats who agree that boys and men in girls' locker rooms are wrong will still vote for the Democrats who implement these policies.

These are the core reasons the distance between Republicans and Democrats has become unbridgeable. It's also why much of the world is this way. A classic example is the Jewish country of Israel and its never-ending conflict with Iran and other surrounding Middle Eastern countries.

Imagine living in a neighborhood where almost everyone wants to kill or seriously harm you. Imagine living next door to someone constantly trying to destroy you. When you try to reason with them, make peace, offer concessions—they still want to eradicate you. Actually living this way would be a real-life nightmare for most of us. This is the reality for the people of Israel.

From the horrific attack on October 7th to suicide bombers, this is what they endure. When they defend themselves, Israel practically has to ask for permission—and then faces endless claims that their response was too brutal. Reality can be far more horrifying than any scary movie.

The attack was mostly on a civilian, unarmed population—with widespread reports of rape, mass murder of adults and children, babies being put into ovens. Much of it was captured on video by the terrorists themselves, who laughed and proudly called family members to brag about it.

This is the very definition of evil in our world—something we all must contend with, whether we realize it or not. Imagine being so brainwashed that you don't know you're on the side of evil. There are endless supporters on college campuses and elsewhere denying, defending, or excusing what Hamas terrorists did that day.

It was the mathematical equivalent of New York City being invaded and approximately 61,500 people being assaulted and murdered—many times worse than 9/11. That would be considered an act of war. What do you think America's response would be? Would we listen to other countries and college protesters telling us we fought back too hard?

The Bible speaks of a time when good would be called evil and evil would be called good. This is the time of moral confusion we now live in—where the moral compass of many is lost. The ability to stand up and boldly say what is right and wrong, decent or indecent, has become like a watered-down drink at your local bar.

Churches, school districts, government officials are afraid and have been infected with this mindset called political correctness. This is what all of us must contend with, whether we realize it or not.

The word "unbridgeable" almost seems too small. But this is the reality for Israel—and possibly, the future of America. A future filled with suicide bombers and terrorist attacks.

The signs are everywhere. If one is paying attention, they're easy to see. We can't agree on even the simplest truths and policies. Open borders are a prime example.

Any country has the absolute right to establish and enforce its borders. We have the right to choose who comes into our country and who does not. Those we allow in should pass background checks and pose no threat to Americans. It is the basic responsibility of any government to protect its people. This should be something everyone can agree on— but not the Democrat Party. Saying such things is now considered racist and cruel.

Can anyone come into your home day or night whenever they want? Don't you have a responsibility to protect your family? If these concepts are important for your home and your family, why aren't they important for the country? These are logical questions, but they fall on deaf ears when talking to Democrats.

It gives me no joy to say this. I grew up Democrat. But most do not know the issues—they are ruled by emotion, often irrational, and sometimes violent. There are endless examples of Republicans being attacked, spit on, having milkshakes and other food thrown at them. Others have been assaulted and even murdered. One example: a teenage Trump supporter was chased and run over with an SUV, killing him in North Dakota. Another Trump supporter was shot and killed in Portland, Oregon.

Where does this blind hatred come from? It's the result of years of brainwashing by the mainstream media, Hollywood, entertainers—even some church pastors. Most are simply beyond reason.

There's an endless line of Hollywood actors, entertainers, rappers, and others who insist on making statements meant to disrespect conservatives. I'm sure most of them think they're being brave when they make derogatory comments about President Trump and other Republicans at award shows—where roughly 98% of the audience are Democrats like themselves. But cowards are what they really are.

Why don't they take these beliefs to Fox News, Salem Radio, or sit across from Black conservatives like Candace Owens, Congressman Byron Donalds, and others? They don't—because they know they'd be shredded like an unwanted piece of paper.

In addition, there are countless average Democrats and low-information voters who constantly want to get in our faces with little to no knowledge of the issues they bring up. They only have a few talking points they've picked up from CNN or some other liberal outlet. When you correct them or try to give them the full story, it's like they've wandered into the deep end of the pool and can't swim. That's usually the point where they start talking loudly, repeat their talking points, and walk away.

It's actually sad to see that what most of them believe is based on utter nonsense or a fraction of the issue.

Some of you may think this is arrogant or outrageous to say. As a Black conservative, I've had these debates many times. When it comes to political subjects, it's often true. Many are intelligent in other areas, but they have little interest in getting the complete story on political issues. They just go with the talking points they get from mainstream media or believe whatever their local news tells them.

Many don't even know that most news stations are staffed by around 95% Democrats. Can they do their job fairly? Yes—but most don't when it comes to political issues. Many are told or pressured not to by their station owners and managers, who are also mostly Democrats.

A good example is the claim that Trump said "racists are very fine people" in the South Carolina tragedy. They were told this by mainstream media and irresponsible Democrat leadership. It was simply not true. It has been debunked and well documented that President Trump was referring to those who had concerns about the removal of Confederate flags and historical statues.

Many who hold this false belief didn't even bother to watch the full video of Trump's statement, where he clearly specifies what he meant. Most of those who have issues with the Confederate flag don't realize that flag only came about as a result of the Civil War. Their true issue is with the American flag itself—the one that truly presided over slavery in America. Ultimately, I believe they will want that removed or changed as well.

As a Black man, I have profound anger and issues with the Confederacy. But the past is history—it cannot be changed. Many of those supposedly outraged about the statues have been driving past them for decades and thought nothing of it. If you tried to stop these people and explain, they wouldn't have time to hear it.

Suddenly, now they are outraged. It bothers them to the very core of their being. They cannot eat, sleep, be happy, or continue their lives until they speak out, protest, and in some cases, forcibly bring these statues down. They cannot rest until we do something about these monuments they previously barely noticed.

Taking away historical statues, flags, or changing the names of schools and sports teams does nothing to change history. There are better solutions—like putting up statues of heroes from that time and naming schools and buildings after them. This could be a wonderful opportunity to teach about historical Black heroes and the full history of America.

The point is: there are far better things we can spend our energy on than protesting statues we claim to be outraged by but ignore every day.

I am a Black man in America. Like many people of color, I was raised as a Democrat. I later became an independent because I don't want any institution or party to take my vote for granted.

Most of my people believe that because they vote 90–95% Democrat, it makes them important to the party. But that's simply not true. Imagine a man in a relationship with a woman who lets him get away with anything—disappearing for weeks, cheating, bringing side chicks home—and there's no argument, no drama, no "smoke," as the younger generation says.

It sounds ridiculous, but that's exactly what people of color have done for the Democrat Party. Black people and others of color believe they have power in the party but in reality, they don't. When Democrats know they have your vote no matter what, you're in their back pocket. In truth, you have nothing.

We are ultimately insignificant to the Democrat Party because they only need us during voting season. They'll do small things, show up in a Black church, and say, "I'm going to fight for you!" But what does that even mean? Fight who? For what purpose? How can the results be measured?

It's political happy talk that means nothing.

Ultimately, I believe the Democrat Party does not want people of color to be successful. They want us swimming upstream with our hands out, saying, "Help us! Help us!" Those in this position have very little time to look around and see both sides of the issue. It becomes easier to just listen to what they're told by mainstream media, FM radio, and Democrat leaders in their cities and states.

It's easier to ignore high crime rates, poor education, higher taxes, and the thousands of Black men, women, and children murdered every year in weekend shootings. It's easier to accept the brainwashing that destroys the ability to think clearly, logically, and without emotion. It destroys the ability to be reasoned with—which only widens the gap between what one chooses to believe and what is actually true.

At a certain point, the distance becomes so great that one can no longer see the other side.

Another reason the gap between right and left is unbridgeable is the Democrat Party's ability to propagandize mass populations—especially minorities. North Korea and other Middle Eastern countries could learn a lot from the Democrat Party. In those countries, people know their brainwashing is mandatory and that resisting it brings consequences.

In a free country like America, this shouldn't be possible—but they've done it. Through mainstream media, poor education, Hollywood, family, music, and other methods, most Democrats are brainwashed without even knowing it. Even worse, through self-appointed leaders and activist groups, they assist in brainwashing themselves.

The Black race has fallen most deeply into this mental plantation—this mind prison. It's very difficult to escape a prison when you don't know you're in one.

Many people say they're open-minded, but the truth is most are not. Truly being open-minded means being willing to admit you're wrong when presented with logic, facts, and reason. That's the key to being open-minded. It's the key that opens the door to your mental prison. You simply need the courage to use it.

Unfortunately, that character trait is in short supply—and always has been.

Speaking the truth to an irrational, ignorant, and often violent Democrat Party comes with a price. Being willing to step into the fire of truth is the cost of courage. I call this *The Fire of Truth* because in many ways, that's exactly what this book is.

It's hot. It will cost you friends, sometimes family, employment. It can bring insults, violence, and even death. Cowardice and self-preservation are much easier pills to swallow—and they cost very little.

Only your integrity.

There is a mindset—a narrative—that is told to Black people from the time we are young. It goes something like this: Democrats are wonderful, Republicans are a bunch of racists, and Trump is Satan—or whoever the Republican figure is at the time. It takes a lot of courage to stand up to all of this. The Black conservative, by far, has the toughest road.

You must be ready to have endless arguments with people who know very few facts about whatever topic they bring up. Most of their arguments center around Donald Trump or Republicans in general. And when they begin losing the argument or run out of the few facts they have, the word "racist" suddenly appears. It's usually an attempt to gain the upper hand while you're forced to defend yourself against that particular accusation.

The other problem with this scenario is that Republicans need to stop running scared from the word "racist." Look these people in the eye and tell them where to go. Meanwhile, Blacks and other people of color are dying in our major cities at an alarming rate every year. The big-city mayors seem to be corrupt, incompetent, or have some combination of both.

Where is Black Lives Matter? Where are all the other self-appointed leaders of the Black community? They are nowhere to be seen. It is only when a white cop gets into a struggle with a Black man or person of color—often someone not following instructions and with a record a mile long—that you ever hear from these organizations.

The fact is the vast majority of Black men, women, and children being murdered on the streets of these major cities every weekend is at the hands of our own. I really wish Black lives mattered to Black people. We murder ourselves at a far greater rate than the KKK or any racist could ever dream of.

The hard truth is that most of these young Black men and women who are killed in confrontations with police would still be alive if they had simply followed instructions. Most police officers are just trying to do their jobs. They are not perfect. Put them in a confrontation where they are being punched, struggling, perhaps fighting for their lives—they are not always going to make the best choices. No one would. The best thing for everyone involved is not to force that decision into their hands.

Yes, this is a Black man writing this—because truth does not have a color. But it does need to be said and heard.

Of course, as a Black conservative saying this, we are often called "sellouts"—by people of our own race who continue to vote for the Democrat Party. The same party that ran slavery and fought a civil war to keep it. The party that denied us an education. That voted against the 13th and 15th Amendments, which freed us and gave us the right to vote. The party of Jim Crow laws and welfare.

So who are the real sellouts?

What would Harriet Tubman and others think of us voting for the political party that enslaved them, beat them, raped them, sold their children, and killed them at will? I've asked these questions in conversations, and what I usually get in return is loud, incoherent nonsense—something like, *That was back then!*

But the passage of time does not erase what was done to Black people by the Democrat Party. Many of us aren't even trying to understand the mindset that time does not erase murder, rape, and other atrocities. The Ten Commandments have no statute of limitations—and neither do these crimes.

There are also many who now want to change the names of our schools because former presidents and many of our Founding Fathers owned slaves. Black people have a unique perspective on this issue. I believe our Founding Fathers were, in many ways, good men in their time—men who did great things and terrible things. This is the condition of all human beings. We are capable of both greatness and horror. In the best-case scenario, the good we do will outweigh the bad.

Judgment Day is where God will judge humanity based on our actions and beliefs. That's what the Bible describes.

As a Black man, I do not excuse the horrors of slavery in America or anywhere else. But changing the names of schools, sports teams, and other institutions does nothing to change history. Our time is much better spent seeing history for what it was—and trying to make things better now and in the future.

I've watched news shows that feature *man-on-the-street* interviews, where reporters walk up and down city streets asking random questions like: "This is the United States of America—how many states are there?" "Who is the Vice President?" "Name one of the states that border Canada." They ask people from all walks of life—older, younger, college students—and sadly, almost no one gets the answers right.

The point is, when I bring up the horrors of American slavery and the Democrat Party that ran it, most people are surprised. In many ways, this is a travesty in and of itself—that the knowledge of our agony, sadness, pain, and devastation, along with those responsible, is not being passed down to later generations.

That knowledge needs to come from the Black community itself—grandfathers and mothers telling their children and grandchildren. The Jewish people are a great example of this. They teach their younger generations about the Holocaust and who was responsible for it. Black people owe it to those who came before us to do no less.

The truth is many Black people who walk around hating the Republican Party don't know that it was Republicans who fought and died in the bloody Civil War to free us—under the direction of President Lincoln. History and the education system describe this war as between the North and the South, which is accurate. But the real truth is that it was between the Republican Party and the Democrats.

Why hasn't it been presented that way? That's a question I've often wondered about—in school and even now.

Everyone is free to feel however they want, about political parties, but we should at least know the historical facts.

Bringing these issues up is like speaking a different language—and maybe we are. The language of truth. The language of common sense. The language of knowing the facts before you confront someone in a debate.

These things shouldn't be too much to ask. It's what you'd expect from someone going in for a job interview, or someone arguing about a bad call in a football or baseball game. But apparently, it is too much to ask.

It's easier for them to get emotional and loud, rattle off whatever point they think they're making, and shut down the conversation by walking away or calling you a derogatory name.

On the conservative side, we must push through this to find some kind of common ground—and hopefully, enlightenment. It's far too easy to sum them up as gullible, brainwashed, or hopelessly lost. I'm a realist, and the fact is, some of them are. But I'd like to think that the majority can be reached if we just present our side calmly—with information, facts, understanding, and reason.

Much like a ship going down in the ocean, we must try to save as many as we can. Giving up should never be an option. Losing hope should not be an option either.

But too many on our side have written off the Democrat Party—and there are many valid reasons to justify it. The amount of damage the Democrat Party and the Biden administration have done to America, and the world is stunning. If someone—or some group—intentionally set out to destroy America from within, they couldn't have done much better.

America and the rest of the world will be feeling the consequences of what they've done for many years—

perhaps decades. Just as Israel and other countries are dealing with terrorist attacks, chaos, and corruption, America will have to deal with this as well. Whether we want to or not.

What the Democrat Party has done to this country is unforgivable.

Republicans and Democrats, red states and blue states—in many ways, we are like a bad marriage in need of a national divorce. Much like any other situation, the parties involved would go to court to handle financial and family issues and then go their separate ways. This particular situation would definitely involve the Supreme Court or some other method.

Most Americans wouldn't want this—but ultimately, it may be our future.

Many great countries and cities throughout world history have risen and fallen. Nothing in this world is infinite. Something isn't great because it lasts forever. In fact, the reality that it can end at any moment is what makes it special, unique, and important.

In the entire history of the world since the beginning of time, there has never been anyone exactly like you or me—

and there never will be again. Life is the very definition of that fact.

America may not be the longest-lasting nation on Earth. Our freedom makes us the greatest country in the world—but it can also be the cause of our destruction. Freedom is a double-edged sword. It allows us to do great things. It also allows us to do foolish things.

When too much damage is done to the foundation of a building, it will eventually collapse under its own weight. The Bible is full of examples of this.

Maybe that's why the gap we're dealing with is so unbridgeable. If we're not speaking the same language—or can't understand one another—it's very difficult to build a better world or a better environment.

Chapter 2 The Coming of Trump

In almost every society, we can look back and find a moment that changed the course of its history—a moment so important or significant that it can only be seen in terms of *before* and *after*. It affected how people evaluated situations, the direction they would take, and ultimately became a defining moment for the soul of that society. What they stood for—or didn't. Who spoke the truth—or didn't. Who had the courage to call out those on the side of evil, whether they realized it or not?

There came a time when we saw the mainstream media—CNN, talk shows like *The View*—for what they really are: extensions of the Democrat Party. There came a time when we realized that just because someone wears a nice dress or suit and sits behind a beautiful news desk doesn't mean they're telling the truth or reporting fairly. Those who are truly mentally awake began to understand that most of these people are Democrats, lack integrity, and are not telling the whole truth—especially when it comes to politics, and often in other areas as well.

There came a time when not only did we stop getting the truth from mainstream media, but we also saw how complicit they were in cover-ups and wrongdoing. Many wonder why podcasts like Joe Rogan's have become so popular. It's because they speak truth, and many of those who are mentally awake no longer trust mainstream media. There are valid reasons and endless examples of misrepresentation and outright lies that justify this distrust.

A good example is the boy in the Trump hat who was accused of badgering American Indian activist Nathan Phillips. That boy was Nick Sandmann, a student at Covington Catholic High School. The viral video showed Sandmann and other students wearing MAGA hats and shirts, standing in a tense encounter with Phillips, who was chanting.

The way it was presented gave the impression that the activist was unfairly confronted and harassed by the boys. Sandmann was called names and disrespected by CNN and other mainstream outlets. But it was later revealed that Phillips had approached the boys and began chanting in their faces. Sandmann, confronted, chose not to turn his back or walk away. Instead, he stood still and smiled—a remarkably mature decision for someone so young.

It was the adults—the mainstream media—who acted immaturely, name-calling and failing to get the facts straight before presenting the story to the public. CNN and other outlets would later settle out of court after a lawsuit was filed. This is what passes for journalism in the age we live in.

Fox News isn't perfect, but they are far better than the alternative. At least, for the most part, you get something approaching integrity and truth. There came a time when the mainstream media should have been embarrassed and ashamed to call themselves journalists and reporters.

There was a moment in time I call *The Coming of Trump.*

I am an independent voter. Like many people of color, I was raised a Democrat. But I've never been afraid to hear either sides of any argument or idea. If we're lucky, many of us will reach a point where we become mentally aware and awake—not *woke*. Mental awareness means having a higher understanding, being quick to perceive, evaluate, and act in a given situation. It helps us avoid blindly accepting whatever is put in front of us.

For example, not walking down a certain street just because others are doing it. Ask: What is the reason? Where is the destination? Why this particular path?

Many fall victim to groupthink—thinking or behaving a certain way simply because others around them are. This is the very peer pressure we warn our children about. In many ways, being mentally strong is harder than being physically strong. Physical strength requires exercise, lifting weights, push-ups, pull-ups. That's it.

Mental strength, however, is an entirely different ball game with vastly different outcomes.

This concept is easy to relate to—we've all been in middle and high school, and so have our kids. The path of least resistance is tempting for everyone, child or adult. I believe it's always been this way, regardless of time or circumstance. In school, following the crowd was the easier path. It came with few consequences. Going along made us accepted, popular, *cool* and maybe even helped us get closer to the boy or girl we liked.

Those things mattered deeply to us then—and many would argue they still do.

But being mentally strong—a free thinker—not blindly following the crowd comes with a much higher risk. It can destroy all the things we think we need and want, whether we're children or adults. The consequences feel just as devastating.

Being an adult gives us better perspective, yes—but pain is pain.

No one wants endless arguments with family members, to lose lifelong friends, or to have coworkers treat them differently. The list goes on. Being a free thinker and mentally strong will give you strength in your soul—but, like many valuable things in life, it comes with a price.

As a child, you may be kicked out of the *cool club* or bullied for not following the crowd. As an adult, the consequences are similar—often worse.

From the beginning of time, there have always been men and women who paid the price for thinking independently. There was a time in history when the highly educated insisted the Earth was flat—and people believed them. Then came Galileo, who claimed the Earth was round and that the sun—not the Earth—was the center of the solar system. He published a book arguing in favor of this.

Galileo was put on trial by the Inquisition, convicted, and forced to publicly renounce his beliefs. He was sentenced to life imprisonment, later commuted to house arrest at his villa near Florence—for the rest of his life.

This is the age we live in now.

Where questions that challenge the narrative—like election fraud—are met with anger, lawfare, and threats of prison.

The Fire of Truth is what I call it. It's the space where Galileo, President Lincoln, Martin Luther King Jr., conservative activist Charlie Kirk, and yes, Donald Trump, among others, have stood. The history of mankind is full of examples of men and women like these—people who spoke truths others didn't want to hear for one reason or another. They were called liars, unstable, evil, delusional, and a host of other names—all in an effort to dismiss, demean, and avoid what was being said.

Courage is often considered the greatest human trait. I mostly agree. But resolve is an underrated trait that I believe is just as important. In the best-case scenario, courage and resolve should work together.

Think of it like driving a car. Torque and horsepower are terms used to describe what propels your vehicle forward. Torque is what gets you moving when you press hard on the gas. Horsepower is what keeps you going. That's the relationship between courage and resolve.

Anyone can have courage for a moment or a short time. Resolve is what makes you stay with it—to see it through. Many of the great men and women we admire could have made a decision or taken action in the moment, then given up when things got tough, uncomfortable, or even deadly. But they didn't. Resolve is what kept them on the path, moving toward their goal or the end result.

It takes a special kind of human being to stand by a truth they believe into the bitter end. Hero and heroine are the names we give these people, and they should be examples for us all to follow.

These famous examples are well known. But there are many people in our own lives who are just the same. If we're paying attention, we can see them taking a stand— sharing opinions and taking actions that some may think are wrong, unreasonable, or simply don't make sense. These people, whether in our lives or in history, are no less heroic than those I've just mentioned.

Their names may not be known. The place where they make their stand may not be large. But if we're paying attention, we'll see that their actions matter just as much as those who are well known or famous.

Whether they're speaking out at a local school board meeting against nonsense policies, or standing by a child, a young man, or a woman who's had trouble with the law but shows potential—these heroes and heroines are all around us. If we just pay attention, we'll see them. And if we open our eyes wide enough, we may find that person is you.

If what you believe can't stand up to questioning, it's probably wrong. That's one of the life lessons I've learned and hold to be true. Whether the subject is political opinion, science, religion, sports, or any other topic, this principle still applies.

When you're justifying or supporting something that can't be logically and rationally defended, it's a sign you're on the wrong side of the discussion. If you're trying to explain or support something and it feels like you're rationalizing the indefensible—it's probably because you are.

Those who become emotional, angry, threatening, resort to name-calling, or walk away from the conversation are essentially saying they have no legitimate argument that makes sense.

Always give yourself the freedom to admit when you're wrong. It takes bravery and character to be strong enough to change your opinion when you gain a better understanding or realization of the issue.

The coward is the one who clings to opinions that are rooted in emotional nonsense—driven by fear of being proven wrong. They stay with their *or else* mindset, which basically says: "Shut up and think as I do. Believe and behave as I do—or else there will be consequences!"

There are endless examples of people being suspended or removed from Facebook and Twitter simply for asking relevant and important questions. Conservatives and their families have been harassed, run out of restaurants and movie theaters. Many have been spat on, physically attacked, and some even murdered.

Freedom of speech, in their view, does not include having an unapologetic conservative opinion—especially on topics like gender-affirming surgeries for minors, open borders, or the fabricated Russia investigation into President Trump.

The New York Post published an exclusive report detailing how the CIA and FBI orchestrated the Russia collusion narrative. A bombshell new CIT review of the Obama administration's intelligence agencies' assessment—that Russia interfered in the 2016 presidential election to help Donald Trump—was deliberately corrupted by then-CIA Director John Brennan, FBI Director James Comey, and Director of National Intelligence James Clapper.

Brennan was excessively involved in drafting the report and rushed its completion through a chaotic, atypical, and markedly unconventional process—raising serious questions about political motives. Furthermore, Brennan's decision to include the discredited Steele dossier over the objections of the CIA's most senior Russia experts undermined the credibility of the entire assessment.

This was all verified by the tradecraft review of the 2016 Intelligence Community Assessment on Russian election interference, conducted by career professionals at the CIA's Directorate of Analysis and commissioned by CIA Director John Ratcliffe.

Additionally, CBS News reported the release of more than 100 pages of declassified files, including a memorandum from the Director of National Intelligence Tulsi Gabbard. She stated,

> "There was a treasonous conspiracy in 2016 committed by officials at the highest level of our government." She also submitted a criminal referral to the Department of Justice.

In the face of all this, why would any American believe anything coming from these individuals about Trump?

The sad truth is that roughly half the country will believe anything the corrupt mainstream media and these officials say. The amount of declassified files, bank statements, and witness testimony from DOJ and Congressional investigations showing many of these people to be criminal and dishonorable hypocrites is staggering.

Most of it will go unnoticed by Americans who are more than willing to confront you with arguments—and sometimes even violence—while they themselves remain uninformed. It's a sad commentary on the state of affairs in this country and many others around the world.

All of it was done for a case that the FBI, CIA, and others knew was false from the beginning. It was disclosed to President Obama in a closed-door meeting, yet he allowed it to proceed. The fake Russia investigation cost American taxpayers roughly $32 million and ruined the lives of over 30 people—all for nothing more than hatred of Trump and an investigation that should never have been allowed.

These corrupt actions from the Democrat-aligned deep state come as no surprise to those of us who think clearly and pay attention.

Raising valid questions about the 2020 election fraud and the mistreatment of the January 6 defendants also led to President Trump being removed from Twitter. Like millions of others, I was threatened on Facebook to "watch what I was posting" about these topics—or face consequences such as suspension or "Facebook jail."

Before Trump came along, the mainstream media, Facebook, Twitter, and the rest at least gave the appearance of being fair and unbiased. Now, all pretense is practically gone.

On CNN, one of their so-called *unbiased* journalists, Don Lemon, called President Trump a racist on a national news broadcast. As reported by the Washington Post, major news networks—ABC, NBC, CBS, and others—cut away from President Trump's speech on November 5, 2020, because they claimed he made unfounded accusations. CNN and NBC also cut away from other speeches, acting as if they were America's nanny.

According to the New York Times, this was done because they felt Trump's remarks were misleading and false. But who the hell are they to decide what the American people should hear from their President or candidate for President?

The American people are not children, and the mainstream media are not our parents. They were elected to nothing. Imagine the arrogance and audacity it takes to believe they have the right to do this.

The American people will listen to what our President has to say—and we will decide whether or not we believe it. Whether or not we think it's true.

Would it surprise you to know that this has never been done to any other U.S. President?

It wasn't done to Kennedy, LBJ, Nixon, Carter, Reagan, Clinton, Bush, Obama, or Biden. No one—but Trump.

This is our so-called *unbiased* media—one that millions of Americans have come to know and despise.

I tended to lean Democrat and voted for Barack Obama. I also voted for Arnold Schwarzenegger for Governor of California. Then and now, I've always seen voting as a rational decision—not an emotional one. The only relevant question should be: Who is the best person for this job at this time?

President Obama was that person for the eight years before Trump came along. And yes, being the first Black president was a motivating factor as well. The candidates he ran against—John McCain and Mitt Romney—made the choice fairly easy. In my opinion, they were weak and feckless, representing everything wrong with the Republican Party and nowhere near a Ronald Reagan-type candidate.

Both McCain and Romney had an impersonal, aloof way of communicating. That may work for some, but there was no real connection with regular people. Most of us who pay attention can sense whether someone is authentic and sincere—for better or worse, this is who they are. Neither of them had it. Their speeches and talking points were like school cafeteria food: bland, no spice, the same thing we've heard over and over again.

Ronald Reagan was the only Republican candidate and president who had anything approaching sincerity. Romney and McCain set the bar pretty low. I was too young to vote during Reagan's time, so I didn't pay much attention. But if I had, I believe I would have listened to what Reagan and Carter had to say and made a decision based on who was best for the position.

I often wonder: Is it better to be smart or wise? Opinions differ, but I've always leaned toward wise—because wisdom implies deeper understanding. For example, I imagine there aren't many wise people in prison, but I know there are plenty of smart ones. When making decisions about our leaders, friends, spouses, or partners, I believe the better choice is always the wise one.

As the presidential primaries continued, I started listening to what all the candidates had to say. Most of them offered the politically correct answers you'd expect—again, much like cafeteria food in middle or high school. Trump was the only one who said things that were true and needed to be said.

Could he have said them in a more politically correct way? Probably. But I noticed that those who were angry with him weren't angry because it was a lie—they were angry that it was said at all. Personally, I prefer blunt truth over being told what someone thinks I want to hear. Trump was that blunt truth.

I'm speaking specifically about illegal immigration, which was the first of many issues the mainstream media and others had with him. They claimed he called all illegal immigrants criminals—a lie the media clung to and spread like wildfire to those willing to believe it. This false claim gave them a reason to throw around words like racist, bigot, rude, and others to justify their dislike and eventual hatred.

While other candidates ran for the hills over illegal immigration, Trump stood his ground without apology and took the heat. Courage is what I saw in him then—and now.

The courage to stand in the fire, speak truth, and fight to defend it.

Thousands of American citizens have been murdered or harmed by individuals who were not supposed to be in our country in the first place. *Angel families* is the term used to describe the loved ones left behind. Truth is not always politically correct.

What was really wrong with what Trump said? Can anyone just walk into your home anytime they want? How can you say you love your family if you allow that? You have the absolute right to decide who comes into your home, your car, or your property—without apology. So does any country. It is the basic job of any government to protect its citizens, and part of that protection is controlling its borders.

Many wonder why Donald Trump really decided to run for president. He had mentioned it a few times on Oprah and other shows. It's often said that the best people never go into politics because it's such a dirty cesspool. Imagine the mainstream media digging into your life—talking to every ex-girlfriend or boyfriend, every person you've broken up with or divorced. What do you think they'd find? What would your ex say about you? What private or awful things would be dragged into the light? Your taxes, your business dealings—everything under a giant microscope.

Courage, love for country, additional fame, or maybe even temporary insanity—whatever the reason, Donald Trump chose to do it. Perhaps it's something like *The Bachelor* or *The Bachelorette* reality show: you do it for fame and fun, not really expecting to win. So what happens when you do?

We may never know the true reason why anyone chooses to enter politics. Whatever the reason, I believe Trump deciding to run was one of the best things for our country— and may very well be its salvation.

Whether you like, love, hate, or despise him—however you feel about Trump—we can all agree that there will never be another like him.

When I first heard that Donald Trump was running for president, like many Americans, I thought it was some kind of joke. Maybe he just wanted to get his name out there in the mix of a national election. The establishment Republicans treated it like a passing fad that would soon be dismissed so we could move on to more *serious* candidates.

The Bush family was considered the serious option, with George Bush's brother Jeb throwing his hat in the ring, along with over a dozen other candidates. Many of them were well known—Dr. Ben Carson, Ted Cruz, and others. But Trump stayed at or near the top of the group and eventually won the nomination.

Another defining moment came when, years before he even ran for president, a tape surfaced of him having a private conversation about women in a lewd fashion. To no one's surprise, most Republicans ran for the hills. Even his running mate, Mike Pence, was nowhere to be seen. Many close to his campaign thought he should drop out.

Trump explained that it was a private conversation, recorded by accident, years before he ran for president— and it was basically *locker room talk*. Once again, the mainstream media and others were outraged.

The key words here are *private conversation* and *years before*. We've all said things in private that we wouldn't want anyone to know. This is for women everywhere: I hate to shock you, but men have these conversations much more than you think. I've heard worse sitting in a Starbucks surrounded by friends. Women do this too—just on a different level.

It's locker room talk.

Most of what men say in those conversations—we assume 50 to 75% of it is nonsense. But we laughed along anyway. As they say, it was much ado about nothing. But it only added fuel to the fire for those with endless Trump hatred.

I often wonder: What is this blind, intense hatred of Donald Trump really about? Do they even know? Are they like the dog chasing the car—not really knowing why?

Most of the people I debate constantly tell me how much they hate Trump, yet they bring him up all the time. They'd never admit it, but I think many of them would have fewer problems with Ted Bundy or some other serial killer.

In the end, I think their real hatred is with us—Trump supporters. We stand by this imperfect man who possesses a strength and courage we've seldom seen, and who speaks truth to those who really don't want to hear it.

To speak a truth that needs to be said—come hell or high water, politically correct or not—means looking the mainstream media in the eye and calling them out for the fake news they truly are. In many ways, this defines Donald Trump in a way that only his supporters can fully understand.

We are living in an age where a man can say he's a woman, compete in women's sports, and win competitions and awards—while most female competitors and authorities are afraid to say how unfair and ridiculous it is. We are in an age where boys and men can walk around women's locker rooms without shame or apology. We are allowing young boys and girls to undergo surgeries such as breast removal, and most of their parents allow it.

This is an act of evil. If you support this, you are on the side of evil. That's not to say you are a horrible person— you simply may not be thinking clearly. But the truth needs to be said.

Unfortunately, objective truth is giving way to *my truth*, which basically means truth is whatever someone says it is. To speak against these things is to be called a racist, a bigot, and a host of other derogatory names.

I have never seen the level of hate for any politician as I've seen for Donald Trump. Once again, it's my belief that as much as they hate Trump, they hate his supporters even more. How can we like and vote for him when Hollywood stars, rappers, and the mainstream media tell us not to? Don't we know they're much smarter and wiser in these matters than we are?

Nothing could be further from the truth.

Most of these entertainers know very little about what they're talking about when they make unsolicited political statements on stage. Most of them will never have to deal with the consequences of their political opinions—such as illegal immigration or soft-on-crime policies—but regular people absolutely will.

Yes, regular people and their families are the ones who suffer the frustrating, sad, and sometimes horrific outcomes of the foolish, inconsiderate mindset forced on us by liberal politicians and other well-meaning but misguided individuals.

Like most methods of learning, examples are necessary to fully understand. There are many heartbreaking real-life stories of theft, assault, rape, and murder—but I'll share just two.

First, the story of Jamiel "Jas" Shaw II of Los Angeles, as reported by ABC, C-SPAN, and other networks. These are the words of his father, Jamiel Sr.:

"On March 2, 2008, my life changed in the twinkle of an eye. One minute I'm hearing my son's voice—'Be right home, old man, I'm right around the corner!'—the next minute, gunshots, and Jas is dead. I saw the hole in his head and blood everywhere. It happened so fast, Jas was still holding his phone. At the same moment, his mother was serving in our military overseas.

The day we buried Jas; LAPD came to my home to tell us they found the killer. For two weeks, local politicians supported us. Every Black politician in LA did too—they even put up a permanent memorial.

Two weeks later, everything changed. We learned the killer was an illegal alien gang member from Mexico, released from jail with a deportation hold, three-gun charges, and an assault and battery on a police officer. The politicians disappeared.

In 2012, we finally had our day in court. The DA proved Jas was murdered because he was Black. The coroner testified that while Jas was on his back bleeding from a stomach wound, his hands were up, and a second bullet went through his hand and into his head. It was also proven that the gang targeted Black males.

You think Obama cared? You think Black Lives Mattered? No. And we all know Hillary was Obama's third term.

Only Trump called me on the phone one day to see how I was doing. Only Trump will stand against terrorists and end illegal immigration."

The second story is more recent and equally horrific: the murder of Laken Riley in Georgia, reported by CBS, CNN, and other networks.

"Laken was a 22-year-old nursing student at the University of Georgia in Athens. On February 22, 2024, she was killed by Jose Ibarra, an illegal immigrant from Venezuela. While on an early morning jog, Laken suffered blunt force head trauma and asphyxiation. Her body was found in a wooded area near Lake Herrick.

Jose Ibarra, 26, had previously been arrested by both federal and state officials in multiple jurisdictions. In September 2023, he was arrested in New York City on charges of acting in a manner to injure a child under 17—but was released."

He also could and should have been arrested in Georgia for shoplifting, but once again slipped through the cracks.

The Biden administration's open borders policy, law enforcement, and the judicial system failed this Georgia student on every level.

Laken bravely fought for her life for roughly 18 minutes against someone bigger and stronger than her—with no rules, no referees, and no timeouts. *Courageously tough,* doesn't begin to describe the kind of person she was—and would have been.

Yes, the Democrat Party has blood on its hands. And they are not alone.

Two promising young people of different races, from opposite ends of the country, paid for these treasonous and reckless policies with their lives. They are not the first— and they will not be the last. That is yet another tragedy. Every government and law enforcement institution involved at every level of these preventable and needless murders should be ashamed.

This has been coming for a long time. It goes far beyond mere disagreements or differences of opinion. It is much deeper.

Anyone can have their favorite football or basketball team. Some may argue whether LeBron James or Michael Jordan is the greatest of all time. At the end of the debate, we can laugh it off and move forward. No one stops being your friend after 20 or 30 years, and no family member refuses to talk to you or come to Thanksgiving dinner over something like that.

But there are endless stories of kids refusing to speak to their parents because they support Trump. Parents and family members are ashamed of their sons and daughters for the same reason. People who avoid sharing their opinions out of love and respect—sitting quietly at the dinner table or in church while others carry on with uninformed arguments against Trump supporters and Republicans in general.

Democrats are not concerned with minor details like love, respect, or keeping the peace at the dinner table. There is an intolerance and arrogance that comes with being a Democrat—where inappropriate and disrespectful behavior is accepted, and there's no shame or expectation of consequences.

It's an unwritten rule: bad behavior is expected from them, and for the sake of peace, conservatives should just tolerate it. Good behavior and taking the high road is the unwritten rule expected from Republicans.

Why is that?

I suppose the answer is that someone has to be the grown-up in the room.

The fact that we have lower expectations of Democrats is an insult to them. The fact that they have lower expectations of themselves is even worse.

An example: anyone can wear a Democrat cap or Obama shirt almost anywhere and expect no problems. But someone wearing a Trump cap or MAGA shirt has a much higher chance of being assaulted—or even murdered. This is not an exaggeration. It has happened multiple times.

Another example: conservatives speaking on college campuses always need security because they're physically attacked, spit on, or shouted down. The reverse almost never happens.

The point is: speaking the truth, sharing your opinion should not be something that puts your safety—or your relationships with family—at risk. But that is the reality of the age in which we live.

For better or worse, this is the new reality of Donald Trump entering politics and running for president. Before he ran, he was famous and widely liked across America. Well-known talk show hosts such as Oprah Winfrey had been friends with him for many years. She regularly invited him onto her show and spoke glowingly about him. She even made multiple visits to his Mar-a-Lago home. Oprah's best friend, Gayle King, attended Trump's wedding.

Other entertainers featured him on their TV shows and mentioned him in their music. His reality show, *The Apprentice*, ran for over a decade. Trump was also a Democrat for many years. Like most Black people and others of color, I started out as a Democrat as well. I eventually became an independent, though I still mostly voted for Democrat candidates.

Like most people, when I first heard Donald Trump was running for president, I didn't take it seriously. I laughed it off when a coworker said he might actually be a great choice. Later, I apologized to that coworker for being wrong.

Unlike many people of color, I wasn't afraid to rethink my position and admit when someone else was right. I was willing to listen to the other side of any argument, and if I couldn't offer an objective response that made sense, I rethought my opinion and was willing to accept theirs.

The comments and statements made by Donald Trump contained a lot of truth. Some would say he could have delivered them with more finesse or a little sugar to help them go down easier—but in the end, truth is truth.

Then I watched the mainstream media misrepresent his comments—like claiming he said all illegal immigrants were killers and rapists. What he actually said was that *some* of them were. Technically, entering our country without permission is a criminal act—much like someone breaking into your home without your consent.

Donald Trump is like the dad or uncle who's blunt but usually correct in what he says. He's not concerned with being politically correct and has the courage to speak without apology. That's refreshing in a political world where most leaders tell you what they think you want to hear and tap dance around tough issues they fear might upset people.

Establishment, RINO, and weak Republicans don't seem to understand that this is exactly why so many people love, like, and respect Donald Trump—and why they're willing to stand in the fire with him. That's why he has defeated every Republican he's ever run against for president. And yet, they still wonder why they lost.

Sometimes I wonder why so many Republican politicians have learned nothing from Donald Trump. Speak the truth about things that need to be said—whether they're comfortable or not, politically correct or not—and be willing to act on it. Have the courage to stand by the truth, and people will follow you.

Democrats will risk everything based on lies and disinformation. Republicans, on the other hand, often have truth, evidence, facts, and figures on their side—but they are as timid as the day is long.

If I had to sum it up in one word, the Republican Party lacks courage.

Perhaps they will never understand what they need to learn from President Trump. If they don't, it will be a travesty— not just for the Republican Party, but for our country as well.

America was not created with cowardice—and it cannot survive with cowardice.

-

Chapter 3: Trump Derangement Syndrome

Trump Derangement Syndrome—a blind, irrational hatred of Donald Trump that surpasses logic, reason, common sense, and love of country. That's my definition, and I think it sums it up well. There should be a serious psychological analysis and study of this phenomenon someday. TDS is not a sarcastic label—it's very real and very dangerous.

It has affected every level of our society, from national to local institutions: Congress, law enforcement, mainstream media, Hollywood, and even other countries. High-level government agencies like the FBI, CIA, DOJ, and others have had their reputations ruined by the biased behavior and actions of their agents and representatives.

It's a strange type of temporary mental illness that takes hold of people—I've seen it up close and spoken with many who suffer from it. People who are normally intelligent and rational suddenly lose all concern for understanding, fair treatment, equal justice, or benefit of the doubt when the topic involves Trump.

Many nationally known individuals from various professions were willing to risk their integrity, careers, and even employment to pursue irrational actions against him. Whether it's political correctness or TDS, it's incredibly difficult to cut through and have a rational conversation with those affected.

Most of their arguments are emotional nonsense, lacking any rational perspective. They believe Democrat propaganda based on little or no factual evidence. The very idea that they might be wrong is like speaking to them in a foreign language—they simply don't understand, and many don't want to.

The fact that millions of Trump supporters are Black, white, Asian, Hispanic, and from all social classes seems to have no effect on their opinion.

I've come to believe that mental clarity is a gift—an ability that almost everyone has, but some will never learn how to use. It's like learning to swim they think they'll never need it, and if they're on a boat, they'll have a life preserver. In this scenario, conservatives like me are the life preservers—keeping them afloat in a sea of emotional nonsense.

Even when hikers wander into forests or mountains and ignore signs or directions, someone has to come help or save them. Perhaps this is our cross to bear as conservatives: to save the ones we can, in essence, to save them from themselves.

The other side of this mental derangement is that some people will never be saved—they're simply too far gone.

A real-life example: the recent tragedy in Texas, where a devastating flood killed over 100 men, women, and dozens of children at a summer camp. The bodies hadn't even been recovered yet when a pediatrician from Houston made despicable comments on social media, essentially saying they were Trump supporters and *got what they voted for*.

Her comments about the victims and their children were cruel and indefensible. In the words of the New York Post, her remarks were *demented and depraved*. She was actually excited by the backlash she received.

There is an insane cruelty from people like her—and from the Democrat Party in general.

After public outrage and the loss of her job, she issued an apology. Whether it was sincere is anyone's guess. When someone apologizes only after being caught or facing consequences, I tend not to believe it. It's like someone apologizing for stealing—but only after they've been caught and are facing justice.

Her cruel and despicable comments go a long way in revealing who she truly is and how she feels.

That same weekend, over 50 people were shot in Chicago, with six killed. Similar numbers occur in major cities every week and month. Where is the outrage? Where are the comments?

The simple answer: it doesn't exist when it comes to Black-on-Black crime. But if a white person or police officer is involved, it's a different story entirely.

Then we see endless outrage, protests, burning buildings, and a parade of so-called Black activists and leaders on news shows giving commentary. This phony outrage and media attention is all that truly matters to them.

They don't care about their professions, decency, or innocent children being drowned. Nothing matters to them but their blind hatred of Trump and those who support him.

I've often thought that Donald Trump possesses a kind of ability—or superpower. It reveals people for who they truly are, or more importantly, for who they are not. It exposes

those who are courageous patriots willing to speak truth—
and those who are cowards pretending to be.

The so-called Republican *Never Trumpers* would rather see
America fail than succeed under Trump, all in the name of
their so-called principles. People like George W. Bush
reportedly voted for Hillary Clinton, along with other
Republicans who claimed to do the same.

Many of those we once thought were tough Republican
heroes were revealed to be cowards—especially when the
topics of open borders or the fraudulent 2020 election came
up.

The normally tough-talking Sean Hannity of Fox News and
Congressman Jim Jordan were asked about the 2020
election being stolen. Their answers sounded like they were
tiptoeing through a verbal minefield and ended with, *I don't
know.*

What was wrong with simply saying, "I believe the 2020
election was stolen, and there's a lot of information, facts,
and statistics that support my opinion"?

Republican governors in Georgia and Arizona should have
demanded full forensic audits—but instead made excuses
and looked the other way. The same story played out with

the Supreme Court, Attorney General Bill Barr, and local officials and media.

The mainstream media, with their so-called journalists and reporters, dropped all pretense of fairness when it came to covering Donald Trump. They were revealed to be exactly what Trump accused them of being: *enemies of the people* when it comes to political reporting.

The Democrat Party was revealed to be far more despicable than we ever imagined.

And those of us who have the courage to stand with Trump were revealed as well.

We know Donald Trump is not perfect—none of us are. But there are far more good things about who he is and what he does than bad. Those of us who can separate personality and emotion from results can see that he has done far more for this country than most people realize—or are willing to admit.

In Trump's first term, he lowered the Black unemployment rate—as well as that of other minorities—to historic lows. He signed the First Step Act, ending mass incarceration in federal prisons. It was designed to promote rehabilitation, lower recidivism, and reduce excessive sentencing. As a result, many people of color were released from prison and given a chance to rebuild their lives.

Median household income for Black Americans and other minorities also increased significantly.

There are a multitude of great things President Trump accomplished—but you'll seldom hear about them. If we had a mainstream media with integrity and fairness, even those who hate him would know this.

Donald Trump will go down as one of the best presidents in American history.

Black conservatives have the hardest path to walk in this political climate. My advice: know your facts, don't make it personal, and present your arguments with the confidence that comes from truth. This is why you must know your facts—because as a conservative, you have to. The other side is held to no such standard.

Democrats often have the luxury of being wrong without needing to apologize for it. They may get loud, emotional, and erratic, but you must remain calm and make your points—using examples or analogies that help explain your position. Always remember it's not the person you're debating that you're trying to convince—it's the people around them. Whether you realize it or not, they're listening. As the conversation continues, more will gather and tune in. They are your true audience.

It's sad to say, but some people are simply lost. They don't see the light, don't want to, and never will. Many will be strangers, coworkers, and even people we love—but this truth applies to all of them. We save the ones we can through enlightenment, reason, and understanding.

Mental prisons are often worse than physical ones—mainly because you don't know you're in one. If you don't know you're trapped, you have no reason to escape. Sometimes it's the overwhelming fear of being wrong about what you believe. Sometimes it's disinformation from those you think know more than you—national or local news, celebrities, family members, even your local church pastor.

God-given, battle-tested common sense should always be your North Star. If what you're being told doesn't align with it, be suspicious. Ask questions. Don't accept nonsense answers. Make better decisions accordingly.

Like many things in life, these words seem simple—and they are, and they aren't. *God-given* is the keyword here. Many have lost their lives or loved ones by ignoring this wisdom. We've all, at one time or another, put ourselves in dangerous situations unnecessarily. Maybe it was getting into a car with so-called friends you knew deep down wasn't a good idea. Maybe it was a young woman deciding to walk or jog alone in a secluded area, ignoring that inner voice warning her.

The point is: whether it's political decisions, life decisions, or national decisions—what is our North Star, if not God and the common sense He gave us?

Is it the Democrat idea of drag queen story hour for children? Grown men kissing on TV? Letting children decide their gender and undergo corrective surgery and medications—with the help of their parents and medical institutions?

Deep down, you know this is unacceptable. Children should not be demanding, planning, or making decisions about things they are too young to understand. These things happen when there is no North Star—or when it's replaced with nonsense.

Speaking truth and common sense without apology may seem simple, but in today's world, it's not. Courage is required to say what is right—whether it's politically correct or not, whether feelings are hurt or not, whether you're hated for saying it or not.

Perhaps unapologetic hard truth is at the core of Trump hatred—a soft lie is preferred over a tough truth. There's a saying: if they're going to hate you no matter what you do, you might as well do what you believe is right.

Democrat brainwashing and Trump Derangement Syndrome (TDS) are close cousins. The difference is that brainwashing is systemic and occurs over time, while TDS is more like temporary insanity. It overrides thoughtfulness, common sense, and rational thinking the moment Donald Trump's name is mentioned. Afterward, they return to their normal selves once the conversation ends. It's quite a sight to behold—and those suffering from it often have no idea what's happening to them.

The Democrat Party excels at one thing: brainwashing mass numbers of people, minorities in particular. This one skill paves the way for everything else. Once your population is brainwashed, you can tell them anything: open borders are great, defunding the police will reduce crime, men who identify as women can compete in women's sports and it's fair. You could even tell them $2 + 2 = 7$—and they'll find a way to believe it.

These things happen when emotion and brainwashing override rational thinking. That's why many of the nonsense ideas coming out of the Democrat Party seem to work in major cities—and why so many independents and conservatives are left shaking their heads in disbelief.

It's why most people in crime-infested cities like New York or Chicago vote around 95% Democrat every two to four years.

To give context: in the first 230 days of 2025, Chicago recorded 254 murders. That's more than one person killed every single day—and that's just one Democrat-run city.

To make matters worse, the mainstream media and the mayor of Chicago claim murders are *on the way down* and refuse federal help—as if that's something to be proud of. Any logically thinking mayor should be begging for help under these conditions.

It's like someone whose life has been awful for years, but things are slightly better at the moment—so they pretend everything's fine.

The people of Chicago and other cities deserve so much better. But the harsh truth is they have to recognize it—and do something about it.

The leaders of these cities have no answers, and they never will—because the problem is them. Their incompetence, no-cash bail policies, soft-on-crime approach, and TDS-driven decisions are the root of the chaos. Everything about their leadership is wrong.

There's a saying: people get the government they deserve. For the sake of these people and their children, I hope that's not true.

If you had a mechanic who kept messing up your car, you'd stop going to him, right? So why, in these major cities with high crime, poor education, and high taxes, can't people see the light? Why won't they vote Republican and give them a chance? They certainly couldn't do any worse.

"What the hell do you have to lose?"

Those were Donald Trump's words—words the mainstream media called racist and insulting simply because he asked a harsh question.

What do Black Americans and other people of color have to lose when every weekend in major cities, men, women, and children are being shot and murdered by the thousands—while incompetent mayors and political leaders offer nothing but meaningless statements and speeches?

They have no plan. No solutions. And they never did.

They are the ones who created these problems in the first place. Their low standards, soft-on-crime and hard-on-police philosophy, high taxes, poor education, and no-cash bail policies have led to the devastation of inner cities.

Another harsh question: how many Black people in these communities will continue burying their family members, suffering through failing schools and broken systems, before they hold their leaders accountable and vote them out?

The harsh answer is they probably never will.

Blaming Trump—or some other white guy—is much easier than looking in the mirror. My answer is simple but tough: more Black people and others of color need to run in these cities as Republicans and speak the harsh truth. Most of them will lose in the early going, but I have to believe and pray that eventually my people will come around, vote for them, and make their lives better.

We do not have to tolerate endless weekends and months of our men, women, and children being killed in our major cities. It is not inevitable. It is not just a fact of life we have to accept. Why is it that so many of us are willing to accept this standard of living from Democrat leaders but refuse to vote for Republicans? Do we really hate them more than we love the safety of our own families?

Why not give them a chance for two or four years? You can always go back to voting for more of the same with the Democrat Party—no matter what they do or don't do for us. It's a free country, after all.

If you're walking in the wrong direction, the first thing you have to do is stop in your tracks, turn around, and start walking the other way. Simple—but tough.

Black Republicans running these cities would bring a completely different mindset and different policies. The victims would be the ones who matter—not the criminals. Black, white, or brown—put enough bad people in prison long enough, and your streets will become safe. Not politically correct, but it's common sense—and it will save untold numbers of lives.

Black, white, or brown—get rid of the bad teachers, hire better ones, and pay them more. The students trying to learn are the ones who matter. Thugs and wannabe gangbangers will be disciplined, suspended, and expelled if necessary. Create a higher level of expectation and hold everyone to it—teachers and students alike—and the education in your schools will improve. Again, not politically correct, but it's common sense. Simple but tough.

Is there racism out there? Yes, there is. So is dust in your home—and if you look hard enough, you'll find that too. The question is: does it stop you from chasing your dreams and goals? The answer is no; it does not.

Blaming Trump for asking a harsh question that should have been asked many years ago is not the answer to our problems. We are the answer to our problems—if we just have the courage to look in the mirror and do something about it.

There is no cavalry coming over the hill to help—because it's us.

Black people in particular need to start thinking clearly and rationally, making the tough decisions that need to be made, and then taking the actions that need to be done. We need to stop waiting for another Martin Luther King to come riding in on a horse to solve our problems.

We are the cavalry. We are the ones who will save our people.

The quote "No one is more hated than he who speaks the truth" is attributed to the ancient Greek philosopher Plato.

Those eleven words describe the blind hatred for Donald Trump more than any others.

I often wonder: why are so many Democrats—and Republican Never Trumpers—so willing to live believing utter nonsense rather than hear uncomfortable truth? Why does truth make them so angry? Or is it really fear?

The fear of being wrong about so many things for so long. The fear of confronting their political choices, life decisions, and lacking the courage and integrity to accept a truth they don't want to believe.

These are serious and defining questions. How we answer them—or don't—says a lot about the kind of people we are.

There's a well-known movie about people living in a world where everything presented to them is false. It's called *The Matrix*. In the middle of it, the hero is offered a choice: the red pill or the blue pill. The red pill reveals uncomfortable truth. The blue pill allows him to keep believing whatever nonsense he's been told.

In many ways, this describes the America we live in today. The choice and knowledge before all of us.

Many educators will tell you that the hardest student to teach is not the one who doesn't know—it's the one who doesn't want to know. Unfortunately, I believe many people of color—and others in America—would take the blue pill and continue believing the nonsense fed to them by the Democrat Party.

The good news is the arrival of Donald Trump, who has made a serious effort to reach out to Black people and others of color.

Meanwhile, one of the Black Lives Matter founders was secretly buying a $6 million mansion. BLM co-founder Patrisse Cullors admitted in an Associated Press interview that she spent nights there and hosted multiple personal parties and events at the Malibu mansion.

Because of examples like this, Black Americans and other minorities are beginning to see the light—and why these organizations seldom, if ever, show up for Black-on-Black crime when lives are lost.

I can see it's starting to change—and that gives me hope for the future.

We also need to be realistic about the plain fact that we're never going to save or enlighten everyone. Some people are simply beyond reason. Rational arguments are useless. We all have people in our lives who fit this description—coworkers, family members, even friends.

There's a term called triage: the preliminary assessment of patients or casualties to determine the urgency of their need for treatment. It's often associated with battlefield conditions—and that's literally what we're in: the battlefield of ideas and rational thinking.

Unfortunately, there are those who simply cannot be saved from their brainwashed ideas, irrational thinking, and blind hatred.

The good news is that some can be saved.

The choices must be hard and fair—but we must make every effort to help people see reason, the light of truth, and common sense.

Many of the people I know suffering from Trump Derangement Syndrome remind me of an ex-girlfriend who claims to hate her former partner but spends all her time talking about him, arguing over him, and wondering what she ever saw in him. Another example is those on Facebook who say they hate everything about Trump but constantly post awful things about him and get into online arguments.

Worse, they actively seek out conservative pages and MAGA Republicans' posts just to start fights.

There are Democrat leaders and even some Never Trumpers I strongly disagree with, but I would never waste my time searching for them online. Don't they have better things to do than trolling conservative sites and dragging others into their rabbit hole of nonsense? It sounds ridiculous and pathetic—but when you think about it, it makes sense.

Before Donald Trump ran for president, many Hollywood stars, professional athletes, rappers, and entertainers were his friends. Oprah had him on her show several times and frequently visited Mar-a-Lago, as did many other celebrities. Trump made guest appearances on numerous TV shows and hosted his own for years. Back then, you didn't see actors like Robert De Niro attacking him on stage at award shows. Politicians like the Clintons accepted campaign donations and socialized with him. Rappers mentioned him in their music. He was interviewed countless times by the mainstream media.

Now, they hate the very ground he walks on. CNN and other networks that claim to despise him spend much of their airtime talking about him. Yes—they're very much like ex-girlfriends. In need of counseling.

I've disliked people and things before, like many of us have. But never beyond logic, reason, and common sense. I would never hate someone so much that I'd put myself or those I care about in danger, or compromise my integrity, professionalism, or financial stability.

High-level FBI agents Peter Strzok and Lisa Page did exactly that. Most of us have heard the recordings of them plotting to derail Trump's campaign, talking about *insurance policies* to ensure he wouldn't stay in office. They were key figures in investigations involving Trump. Once considered professionals with solid reputations, they're now punchlines.

Then there were the 51 members of the intelligence community who signed a letter claiming Hunter Biden's laptop had all the hallmarks of Russian disinformation— despite the FBI already having the laptop and knowing the claim was false.

Another example: the fake Russia investigation, which began with a fraudulent dossier paid for by Hillary Clinton and the DNC to cover up her email scandal.

Among the worst offenders are journalists and so-called reporters whose actual job is to find and report the truth—to present both sides in an unbiased fashion. I understand that talk show hosts and late-night comedians offer personal opinions. But news people are supposed to operate on a higher level.

Yes, most of them are Democrats. But they're supposed to be professional enough to report the news fairly and without bias. Unfortunately, most of them don't.

This failure exists on both the national and local levels. I'm sure that when many of them entered the profession, some part of them genuinely wanted to report the truth—follow the clues, chase the evidence, and tell the story. They didn't say, "I'll report the truth until my supervisor tells me not to."

I miss the days when reporters chased down corrupt politicians, shoved microphones in their faces, demanded answers, and investigated stories—consequences be damned. Yes, I understand they need their jobs and the money is good. But at some point, you're either a journalist or you're not.

Why didn't they say, "I'm going to report both sides of the fake Russia investigation, the 2020 election fraud, Joe and

Hunter Biden's foreign dealings with China, Ukraine, and Russia, their shell companies, and the lawfare against Trump"?

These are questions that go to the core of whether we have a free, honest, and fair press in America—or not.

They have failed the American people on every level. These should have been the biggest stories of their careers—some of the biggest stories in American history involving corruption. Many of these news hosts, journalists, and reporters should be embarrassed and ashamed. If they had any real integrity, they would apologize to the American people and resign—making room for professionals who actually have courage and aren't suffering from TDS.

When most Americans turn on the TV and see these anchors behind beautiful desks in professional suits, they assume they're being told the truth. This is the most insidious betrayal of all—being misled by those whose job it is to tell the truth and present both sides.

It reminds me of a quote I once read: "The people, being more or less ignorant and corrupt, get the governments they deserve." That statement comes from French writer Joseph de Maistre. Years later, former President Barack Obama echoed it, saying, "You get the politicians you deserve."

I've come to believe these statements apply to the mainstream media as well.

Americans give the media far too much credit and trust—especially when it comes to presenting both sides of the issues. Like any other institution in America, they need to be held accountable and face consequences for failing to meet expectations.

It's almost impossible to convince people they're being fed biased nonsense—especially when it comes to political issues—by these so-called news professionals. Even after national shows like *60 Minutes* and *ABC News* had to pay out millions in lawsuits brought by Trump, many still refuse to see the truth.

There are endless examples of these so-called professionals destroying their integrity and careers because of the blind, irrational hatred known as Trump Derangement Syndrome.

Chapter 4: The fraud election of 2020

Many believe the 2020 presidential election was indeed stolen—and I believe history will prove us right. Democrats, weak Republicans, federal agencies, and even foreign governments were likely involved. The fact that something like this could happen in America is so terrifying that most people would rather bury their heads in the sand than face the truth in the plain light of day.

God willing, when a proper investigation is finally conducted and all the facts are known, we—and others—will look back at this time and see the ugly truth. The 2020 election will go down as one of the worst acts of treason in American history, carried out by those who believed they knew better than the American people and that their will should override our votes.

As American citizens, we have the absolute right to fair elections that can be verified. If you had an accountant or cashier who told you they couldn't verify how much money was in the register—or didn't care how much of it was counterfeit—you'd fire them on the spot.

This isn't solely about President Trump. There are many ways the Democrat Party has manipulated elections: counting illegal immigrants in the census, issuing driver's licenses to them in states like California, which is the first step toward enabling illegal voting.

Gerrymandering—defined as the political manipulation of electoral district boundaries to advantage a party, group, or socioeconomic class—is another tactic. Simply put, it's just one more way the Democrat Party has used to win elections for Congress and other offices.

The United States Congress is supposed to be representative of the population from each state. Would you be surprised to learn that nine states with Republican voting populations ranging from 25% to as high as 45% have zero Republican representatives in Congress? That's mathematically impossible for any logically thinking person—but it's the reality of what's been done.

The way these states draw their districts, along with other methods, is yet another way Democrats have abused our electoral system. This needs to be exposed in the plain light of day—just like what happened in the 2020 election.

This isn't about *moving on*. In future elections, we need to know that our country is truly being run by the will of the people. If that's not the case, then we don't live in a free country—we live under a Democrat dictatorship.

When a political party promotes bad or nonsensical ideas, ignores laws, and shows no concern for consequences, it only makes sense that they would resort to stealing elections. High-level government officials and others who can't win legitimately—and who fear no accountability— see this as a valid option.

I use the word "treason" carefully. One definition is the act of betraying one's country by attempting to overthrow the government. Another is an illegal and overt attempt by military or government elites to unseat incumbent leadership. While definitions involving military action or violence don't apply to the 2020 election, the betrayal of the American people certainly does.

The point is this: the Democrat Deep State and its allies are capable of anything. And the Republican Party still has no idea who they're dealing with.

Republicans simply cannot bring themselves to believe that their fellow Democrats are capable of this level of treasonous behavior. They think if we just appease them and appeal to their *higher nature*, a compromise can be reached. The problem is, many of them have no higher nature—even when they claim to.

The hard truth is this: the Democrat Deep State is carrying out this corruption, and the rest of their party consists of low-information voters who either don't know or don't care.

Either this country is run by the will of the people—or we no longer live in the land of the free.

In this chapter, we will go over the facts, the available information, and the results of election audits that were permitted—along with other evidence that defies common sense. The claim that Joe Biden received 81 million votes, more than any candidate in American history—including President Obama, Hillary Clinton, or Bill Clinton—is staggering. A mountain of data, audit results, figures, and anomalies suggest that such a result is mathematically impossible without cheating or manipulation. Any decent mathematician would say the numbers simply don't add up.

Beyond the hard evidence, the behavior of Democrat officials and corrupt or weak Republicans also reveals the truth. Imagine playing cards with someone you know, and you notice they're winning in a way that seems impossible. You ask to see the cards, and they get agitated, scoop them up, and disappear into another room. They return shortly, saying everything is fine—but they don't have all the cards. They claim some were lost, can't be found, and refuse to let you help search for them.

At that point, their behavior tells you everything you need to know. Finding the missing cards becomes a formality. This is the behavior of the Democrat Party and others who label people *election deniers*. One would think they'd welcome a full election audit—machines, routers, everything—if only to prove Republicans wrong and rub their noses in it.

The mainstream media hosts and commentators could go on their shows and gloat endlessly about how they proved Trump wrong with an authentic forensic audit. Instead, they do the opposite: they run the other direction, hide behind lawsuits, suspend people from Twitter and Facebook, and drag their feet to run out the clock. Their behavior alone says it all.

Let me be clear—this is not about Republicans or Democrats. In this country, "consent of the governed" is a phrase found in the 1776 Declaration of Independence. Thomas Jefferson's words were influenced by the ideas of

John Locke. Of all the powerful words and paragraphs in that document, those four words are among my favorites.

"Consent of the governed" is an expression of freedom, equality, and justice. Without it, we are not America—the land of the free and the home of the brave. Consent means our permission, our power, our approval. In short: our votes.

The most powerful thing we have as American citizens is our vote. Nothing else matters if our vote doesn't matter. Our goals, our laws, our policies, our dreams, and the safety of those we love mean nothing if our vote is compromised.

There is a serious problem when a government refuses to prove or verify to its people that it holds power legitimately. That is the behavior of third-world countries and dictatorships. How can we lecture other nations about their elections when our own government uses mass mail-in ballots and voting machines to confuse, conceal, and deceive?

It's the art of making something simple—like voting—complex, confusing, and unverifiable. It ends with the public being told to "just trust us." Excuses, legal maneuvering, and delay tactics are used to deny any real audit or verification.

Tyranny is the word that comes to mind.

Most countries around the world have outlawed mass mail-in ballots and voting machines. They rely on hand-counted paper ballots, voter ID, and mail-in ballots by request only—with ID and a valid reason. That is the only true way to hold an election that can be verified, recounted, or audited if necessary. It's the only way the true will of the people can be expressed.

Our votes decide the direction we take, how we get there, who we choose to protect and lead us—and just as importantly, who we choose not to. Our votes decide—not those who believe they know better and think their will should supersede ours.

This may be the very reason we became America.

This is why our elections are far more important than the average American realizes. Like many decisions in life, voting must be a rational choice—not an emotional one. If you needed heart surgery, would you choose the surgeon whose personality you liked better, or the one who was more capable? If you were boarding a plane, would you choose the pilot based on charm or skill?

To any logically thinking person, these are rhetorical questions.

The ugly truth is that most Democrats vote from emotion, and they have a long history of manipulating elections. This is why they cannot see the truth about the most corrupt presidential election in American history. I know this because I used to be one of them.

After having these discussions many times, I've come to realize that evidence, facts, and figures often make no difference—because that's not the real issue. The real issue is having the courage and integrity to accept a truth they simply don't want to believe.

To my Democrat friends: in the end, you will have to choose between your God-given, battle-tested common sense—or the utter nonsense fed to you by Google, Facebook fact-checkers, mainstream media, CNN, MSNBC, *The View*, and others.

These are the same people who told us the fake Russia investigation was real, and Hunter Biden's laptop was not—because 51 intelligence experts claimed it had "the earmarks of Russian disinformation." These are the same people who couldn't tell us whose cocaine was found in Joe Biden's White House, where only family members and high-level staff are allowed. "We may never know" was one of the empty responses offered.

In an age of video surveillance, DNA testing, fingerprint analysis, and other investigative tools, this is inexcusable.

College degrees, professional titles, sitting behind a news desk, or being called an *expert* does not automatically translate to intelligence, knowledge, common sense, or truth. We've heard countless statements from news anchors like "Trump's false claims of election fraud," as if they've conducted a comprehensive investigation—when in reality, they've done next to nothing.

They've demanded no real answers from government or election officials about data and statistics that simply don't add up.

The 2020 election was going as expected for President Trump. He was ahead by tens of thousands of votes late into the evening. Then, suddenly, swing states stopped counting ballots—roughly around the same time—for no apparent reason. Atlanta, Georgia, used the excuse of a leaking water pipe that caused no real damage and affected no ballots or counting ability.

Isn't it interesting that in the entire state of Georgia, the water pipe burst in the Fulton County election center? Not the week before, not the week after—but on election night itself?

During the overnight hours, ballot drops began arriving, and vote counts for Joe Biden surged in ways that any decent mathematician would say are statistically impossible without cheating. Many of these ballots came in at around 90% for Biden. Many had only a vote for president, leaving the rest of the ballot blank. Many mail-in ballots had no fold—meaning they couldn't have been mailed in an envelope and returned by a voter.

Dozens of firsthand eyewitnesses signed affidavits stating they saw these unfolded ballots. A truck driver signed affidavits and testified to transporting ballots from New York to Pennsylvania. Others reported suspicious and inappropriate activity.

There is also the now-famous video from Georgia showing ballots being pulled from under tables after vote watchers were sent home. The footage shows ballots being scanned multiple times. Of course, explanations were offered—but they defy common sense. Claims that this was "not unusual" or "just a misunderstanding" are utterly ridiculous.

Imagine this: I'm in a bank with six others. Three of us are counting money, and the other four are verifying. At some point, I announce we're done for the night, and we all leave. Later, I return with two others, without telling anyone, and continue handling the money for hours. The next day, I said nothing. Weeks later, a video surfaces showing our behavior.

Now take politics out of it. What does your common sense tell you?

In any other setting, with bank procedures violated and suspicious behavior caught on video, the police would be called, investigations launched, and arrests likely made.

In the turmoil that followed, a lawsuit emerged between Rudy Giuliani and two election workers over accusations and whether something was a flash drive or lipstick. My position: that's beside the point. Those who focus on that are missing the big picture.

The real question is: what were they doing there under those circumstances in the first place?

If you don't want to be accused of suspicious behavior, then conduct yourself in a way that's above board. To this day, there has been no true investigation into the circumstances of that event. Law enforcement and Georgia officials show little interest in pursuing it—which raises serious questions.

The fraudulent 2020 election, involving multiple states, should have been one of the biggest news stories in American history. But the mainstream media chose to ignore it or bury their heads in the sand.

Yes, most of the media are Democrats. But even so, they should want to do their jobs—seek the truth behind the greatest, most corrupt, and treasonous scandal of our time. They should be embarrassed and ashamed to call themselves journalists and reporters. If they had any real integrity, they would apologize to the American people and resign.

But I don't think we're in any danger of that.

In this sea of cowardice and corruption, there are a few boats of courage: Mike Lindell, Kari Lake, Lou Dobbs, and other podcast hosts and conservative media personalities. They were willing to call this out, stand in the fire of truth, and take what came.

And what came was everything.

Suspension from Facebook, Twitter, and other platforms. Lawsuits designed to financially destroy them and ruin their careers. This is the kind of thing you see in third-world banana republics.

In Mike Lindell's case, it's even more remarkable—because it wasn't his job or responsibility to expose the corruption of the 2020 election. That job belonged to government officials, law enforcement, and the mainstream media. And they failed America on every level.

From national to local, most officials and agencies did next to nothing.

If President Obama had run and supposedly lost under these circumstances, there would have been national outrage—and rightly so. Multiple investigations. Full forensic audits with machines and routers. The mainstream media would have done their jobs. America would have gotten to the bottom of it and made corrections to ensure it never happened again.

That is the real travesty of the 2020 election: that none of this was done.

And the consequences will be felt in America for many years to come.

The investigative film *2000 Mules* was a game changer. It exposed a massive, coordinated network of fraud across all five swing states that decided the 2020 election. The film presents two types of evidence: first, geo-tracking data that monitors the cell phone movements of mules—paid traffickers delivering illegal ballots to mail-in drop boxes; second, video footage obtained from official surveillance cameras installed by the states themselves.

This film takes you to the scene of the crime again and again, showing the mules at work. It documents what many believe to be the biggest heist in American history and offers decisive insight into who really won the 2020 election.

The Arizona audit was conducted after extensive foot-dragging and excuses from Maricopa County officials. Over 100,000 man-hours were invested in processing 2.1 million ballots by hand. Each ballot was examined using high-quality DSLR cameras and microscopic imaging of both the front and back.

Here are just some of the findings:

- The canvass showed over 3,400 more ballots were cast than recorded.

- Over 9,000 more mail-in ballots were received and recorded than were officially sent out by the county.

- 2,382 voters cast ballots in person in Maricopa County after moving out of the county.

- Precincts showed 1,551 more ballots cast on election day than people who showed up to vote.

- Approximately 2,500 ballots appeared in early vote returns with no voter listed as casting them.

- Over 255,000 early votes in the county's final vote file had no corresponding entry in the early voting returns file.

- More than 23,000 people voted by mail after the October 5th cutoff date—and those votes were counted.

Keep in mind, Joe Biden supposedly won Arizona by just 10,457 votes.

There was also evidence of voter information being deleted well before federal law allowed it. These are just findings from one swing state—others were reportedly worse.

Summing up the audit: there was an unprecedented number of discrepancies in the vote totals. This could only happen through malicious actions or severe incompetence from Maricopa County officials. The number of questionable votes was more than enough to overturn the 2020 election multiple times in Arizona alone.

The counterargument from Arizona Democrats and weak Republicans is that the numbers pretty much confirmed the vote totals for a Biden victory. That's like saying the money in the cash register matches what the computer says—without checking if the money is counterfeit, valid, or if the computer itself is accurate.

Remember, all these discrepancies were found by carefully processing ballots by hand. Investigators were not allowed to examine the voting machines or routers—both of which are essential for a full audit. Most efforts to investigate the machines have been met with lawsuits, denial, misinformation from mainstream media, and resistance from state officials. What we've seen is foot-dragging, possible corruption, or just plain cowardice from government and state leaders.

In the interest of fairness, it was reported by *The New York Times* and other outlets that *2000 Mules* filmmaker Dinesh D'Souza issued a statement apologizing to a Georgia man who was falsely accused of ballot fraud in the film. It turned out he was legally dropping ballots for a few family members. True the Vote, the conservative election organization that partnered in producing the film, issued a statement affirming that the film's central premise remains accurate despite the apology.

Investigations are not flawless. Even when conducted with care, mistakes happen. In any murder investigation or serious crime, there are always suspects—some of whom may later be cleared. There are often multiple levels of involvement, from prime suspects to those simply present at the scene.

Keep in mind, this was a multi-state investigation involving thousands of suspects. Perfection is a high bar—but in my opinion, they did well. It's telling that out of thousands of mules, only one person was falsely accused. Yet the mainstream media portrays this as if the entire film has been debunked.

Ultimately, you must decide what and who to believe—just like in many areas of life. I choose to believe this investigative film was accurate. To deny it is to deny your own common sense.

Once again, the same mainstream media that told us the Russia investigation was real are now telling us the 2020 election fraud didn't happen. Their track record—especially where President Trump and the Republican Party are concerned—is one of consistent failure, bias, and corruption.

The investigative film *2000 Mules* remains one of the most visual and accessible ways to understand the fraudulent and criminal activity surrounding the 2020 election. The worst part? It's just the tip of the iceberg. As shown in the Arizona audit, other swing states were just as bad—if not worse.

There is a mountain of evidence, facts, and figures that more than validate claims of massive fraud, treason, and criminal activity in 2020. Still, there are those who cannot—or will not—see the truth.

You can always tell when someone doesn't have a valid argument. Critics of the film often say that in some states, it's legal to deliver a ballot for an immediate family member. That's true. The keyword here is *family member*. But let's indulge that argument—say you have seven relatives. What possible explanation could justify delivering 50 to 100 mail-in ballots to different parts of the city, often in the middle of the night, as seen in surveillance footage?

Then returning to non-governmental organization centers to pick up more ballots?

Paying mules to deliver ballots is illegal in all 50 states. They were being paid, and most were not delivering for family members. Through cell phone tracking, investigators could determine the time, dates, and locations these mules visited—some going to as many as 40 to 50 drop boxes.

A conservative estimate suggests that 400,000 illegal ballots were delivered this way—more than enough to change the outcome of the election. The real number is likely double that, since the film didn't count mules who visited fewer than ten drop boxes.

All of this is documented in the movie, leaving little doubt for any logically thinking person. At some point, the excuses run out—and Occam's Razor becomes the only explanation left. It's a problem-solving principle that states: the simplest explanation is usually the best.

Recent reports and hundreds of declassified FBI documents shared with Congress suggest China's involvement in a scheme to influence the 2020 U.S. election. Between January and June of 2020, U.S. Customs and Border Protection officers seized nearly 20,000 counterfeit driver's licenses at Chicago's O'Hare International Airport. The majority—19,888—originated from China and Hong Kong.

This seizure was linked to an FBI investigation into alleged Chinese interference in the election. These are the facts—and they are undisputed.

These fake driver's licenses were sent in the ramp-up to the 2020 election—by China, which has allegedly funneled millions of dollars to Joe Biden through his son using multiple shell companies, as congressional investigations have shown.

What other practical reason would China have to send these licenses at that particular time?

And remember—this is just what U.S. Customs caught. How many more tens of thousands slipped through undetected?

How much longer will those who believe the 2020 election was legitimate continue burying their heads in the sand?

In addition, as reported by John Solomon of *Just the News*, a confidential human source told FBI counterintelligence in the summer of 2020 that China's Communist government was shipping fake driver's licenses to the U.S. to manufacture tens of thousands of fraudulent mail-in ballots for Joe Biden. This was documented in a raw intelligence report distributed to federal agencies.

The report, sent by FBI official Kash Patel to Senate Judiciary Committee Chairman Chuck Grassley, was circulated to U.S. intelligence agencies on August 24, 2020, as an uncorroborated advisory. Then, suddenly, it was recalled—with little explanation other than the Bureau wanted to re-interview the source.

The recall notice specifically instructed agencies to erase or delete the original memo:

"This report was recalled in order to re-interview the source. Recipients should destroy all copies of the original report and remove the original report from all computer holdings."

Officials told *Just the News* that the recall prevented the FBI and other agencies from fully investigating allegations that Beijing was trying to meddle in the U.S. election to benefit Biden—even though corroborating evidence had already come in from another law enforcement agency.

Remember, this recall came after the seizure of nearly 20,000 fake driver's licenses from China.

The original report also stated:

"In late August 2020, the Chinese government had produced a large amount of fraudulent United States driver's licenses that were secretly exported to the United

States. The fraudulent licenses would allow tens of thousands of Chinese students and immigrants sympathetic to the Chinese Communist Party to vote for the U.S. presidential candidate Joe Biden, despite not being eligible to vote in the United States."

Breaking all of this down, almost any logically thinking person would conclude that China assisted in the fraudulent 2020 election. Even after U.S. Border Patrol discovered nearly 20,000 fake licenses, higher-ups at the FBI sent a recall notice to ignore and delete the intelligence.

The corruption within the FBI, other agencies, and a complicit mainstream media is so thick, it's a miracle that any of us can breathe without choking on it.

I believe, deep down, most Democrats know the truth about 2020—even if they may never have the courage to admit it. It takes honor and decency to say you were wrong about something you desperately wanted to believe.

But when the evidence and facts have piled up this high, to deny it is simply to deny reality.

If all this weren't enough, there is a mountain of additional evidence. Fox News and Tucker Carlson reported on vote counts being taken from Trump and given to Biden in Georgia. Surveillance footage obtained by Voter GA—a nonprofit focused on election integrity—appears to show votes being counted multiple times. When asked how many of these votes were counted, Fulton County officials gave no answer.

One way to verify the count is by examining the audit tally sheets. For months after the election, Fulton County failed to provide over 100,000 of these sheets, including 50,000 from mail-in ballots. When Voter GA legally forced the county to turn some of them over, the results were stunning.

Seven falsified audit tally sheets were discovered, containing fabricated vote totals. For example, a batch with 59 actual ballot images for Joe Biden and 42 for Donald Trump was reported as 100 for Biden and zero for Trump. Another example: seven batches of ballot images with 554 votes for Biden, 140 for Trump, and 11 for Jo Jorgensen were falsified to show 850 votes for Biden and zero for both Trump and Jorgensen.

In the Fulton County recount of mail-in ballots, a whistleblower who participated in the process took photos of ballots with no creases—meaning they were never mailed to voters and returned. The whistleblower also stated that the ballots were filled out by printer, not by hand, and contained votes only for Democrats.

Additionally, an election expert analyzed data from the U.S. Postal Service and found that 35,000 voters who had moved out of their county more than a month before the election were still allowed to vote in that county. They should have been ineligible. It was illegal—and those votes were counted.

Remember, Joe Biden supposedly won Georgia by fewer than 13,000 votes.

Atlanta News First also reported that Fulton County officials admitted they did not properly sign tabulator tapes after the 2020 election, a violation of state regulations. The county also noted it had misplaced other tabulator tapes and documents related to the election. The admission was made by County Attorney Ann Brumbaugh during a December 9, 2025 meeting of the State Elections Board.

Tabulator tapes are essentially receipts printed from ballot-tabulation machines that help verify that the number of voters matches the number of votes. They are a key part of the verification and certification process in every county election across the state. Georgia regulations require that a poll manager and two witnesses be present for the printing, checking, and signing of each tape.

More concerning, the unsigned tapes—around 130 of them—accounted for approximately 315,000 early votes in 2020, representing nearly every ballot cast before Election Day. Georgia Secretary of State Brad Raffensperger downplayed the issue, referring to it as a "clerical error."

Garland Favorito, who leads the election-watchdog organization *VoterGA*, offered a different perspective. He stated:

> "A clerical error could be one tabulator tape not signed or one tabulator tape missing—not 148 tabulator tapes missing. I would put it this way: if I called you by mistake once or twice, I could say, 'Sorry, wrong number,' or 'I am confused.' But if I call you 148 times, that is a decision."

I could go on and drown you in even more evidence, but I'll sum it up:

We have video footage from Georgia state cameras showing ballots being taken from under tables by vote counters who left with everyone else, then returned without the rest of their group and stayed for hours counting ballots.

There are also serious questions about voting machines. Georgia candidate Michelle Spears, who ran in the 2022 midterms, had no Election Day votes recorded in nearly 40 precincts—including her own—despite receiving over

2,000 early votes. After she reported the issue, it was discovered she was shortchanged by 3,792 votes due to what was called "technical errors."

What can happen by error can happen on purpose.

It was demonstrated in a Georgia courtroom that vote totals on a machine could be changed with the use of an ink pen. This is why voting machines must go. We need hand-counted paper ballots, voter ID, and mail-in ballots by request only for valid reasons.

Anyone running a business will tell you: if your numbers don't add up, you audit the cash register and inventory systems to verify what's going on.

Some of the questions we should be asking are:

- Why doesn't the Democrat Party support election procedures that can be verified?

- Why do they insist on mass mail-in ballots being sent to everyone, whether requested or not?

- Why do they defend voting machines that many members of Congress—on both sides—have criticized in previous hearings?

- Why do we tolerate vote counting that drags on for weeks or months?

Why do we accept this convoluted and confusing election process, which I believe is designed that way on purpose?

The United States can put a man on the moon and a rover on Mars—but we can't figure out how to run a verifiable election?

These are serious questions every American should be asking—and demanding answers from their government.

There's no urgency to fix this system so we can have free and fair elections. The Democrat Party has a history of cheating, so I wouldn't expect them to care. The Republican Party must be the one to act—with urgency—to restore election integrity.

This is the bottom-line endgame if we truly want to save our country.

Most criminal convictions are based on circumstantial evidence. While it doesn't directly prove a fact, it becomes powerful when combined with other evidence to form a strong case. The reality is that most murders and serious crimes aren't committed on video, with eyewitnesses and confessions laid out for police.

In this age of technology and TV detective shows, we're used to having everything served on a silver platter. But in real life, we must use logic and common sense to determine what is more likely than not.

In law, a "preponderance of evidence" means something is more likely true than not. It's the standard used in most civil cases—greater than a 50% chance of being true.

In my opinion, we're well over the 95% threshold with the fraudulent 2020 election.

With everything I've laid out—and much more that could fill another book or two—we don't suffer from a lack of evidence. We suffer from a lack of courage.

From the mainstream media, Congress, law enforcement, the court system, state governors, secretaries of state—even the Supreme Court—our institutions have failed America on every level.

Elections have consequences. Fraudulent elections have worse.

Millions are dead because of the Ukraine war, open border policies, fentanyl flooding into our country, and the October 7th attack on Israel. The fraudulent 2020 election is at the root of it all.

America will suffer—and many more unnecessary lives will be lost in the years to come—because of the decisions made by the fraudulent Biden administration.

They behaved exactly as if they were a thief in a stolen car.

And that car was America.

Chapter 5 Assassination Attempts

The years following the fraudulent 2020 election were painful and dangerous for the country. The Biden administration was illegitimate—and that's exactly how they behaved. From turning the Justice Department into a political weapon to using lawfare against opponents, they operated more like a secret police than a constitutional government. The examples are endless—from the violation of the constitutional rights of the J6ers to the relentless targeting of President Trump himself.

In life, there are lines you simply do not cross—because once you do, there's no going back. It's called the point of no return, meaning it's further to go back than to continue forward. Some lines are so deep and significant that they can never be forgotten—and may never be forgiven. It's like committing a terrible crime such as murder: some things cannot be undone. Many criminals have said that after the first one, the next becomes easier—with less shame or regret.

This mindset applies to the modern-day Democrat Party in many ways.

Open borders. No cash bail. Prosecutors funded by George Soros with a soft-on-crime philosophy. These policies have resulted in thousands of lives lost—through violent crime, fentanyl overdoses, and other tragedies. Angel families are being created—families whose loved ones were murdered or harmed by illegal immigrants or repeat offenders with dozens of prior arrests who were released again and again.

The Biden administration admits that 10 million illegal immigrants have crossed our open border. The real number is likely double that. Basic math and common sense tell us this has placed the country in grave danger. Even if just one percent of these illegal immigrants are terrorists, that's 100,000 jihad-minded individuals walking freely in America—planning God only knows what.

And the worst part? These numbers are conservative.

Too high for your comfort? Cut them in half. Is 50,000 better for you? Keep in mind: 9/11 was carried out by just 19 terrorists.

There's no way to predict the horrors that could unfold or the lives that will be lost—all so the Democrat Party can flood the country with illegal immigrants who will most likely vote Democrat. Their plan is to fly them to swing states and turn them blue. If this scheme succeeds, fair and free elections by American citizens will be over.

The Democrat Party has blood on its hands—but some Republicans do as well. Republican governors, congressional staff, law enforcement—many were too afraid to speak out or investigate the fraudulent 2020 election. There are moments in history when failing to act turns a manageable problem into a catastrophe. Like cancer, it spreads.

That election, the lack of courage, the hatred of Trump, and the decisions made by the fraudulent Biden White House are at the core of the hundreds of thousands dead due to open border policies, crime, and fentanyl. Angel families now share horrific stories of loved ones attacked, raped, and murdered—stories that have become tragically common.

This is the cost of doing business for those flooding the country with illegal immigrants—actually flying them in at taxpayer expense, then spreading them across the nation to do one thing: vote Democrat.

There's plenty of blame to go around. But the entity chiefly responsible for allowing our country to be openly invaded over four years is, without question, the Democrat Party—

with the corrupt Biden administration facilitating and enabling it.

They are also responsible for the fake Russia investigation and the rest of the deep state shenanigans. Treason—that's the word that fits. And it's not just my opinion. Former Director of National Intelligence Tulsi Gabbard and others with the credentials to know have echoed similar concerns.

This is, without a doubt, one of the biggest scandals and crimes in the history of the United States. And half the country either doesn't know—or doesn't want to.

I often wonder: what was really going on during this time? What were those involved contemplating if Trump won in 2024? Those running the Biden administration must have been making calculations—either to protect themselves or to eliminate the threat altogether.

With everything they've done to Trump, his family, and those in his orbit—through corrupt agencies and investigations—they must have known justice was coming. Could they trust those around them to stay quiet? Was their blind hatred of Trump strong enough to risk shame and prison?

I think not.

Whatever was on the horizon, those involved had to start making decisions for self-preservation. The arrogant ones likely planned to stick it out. The fearful ones probably considered fleeing abroad. They may have thought: "If it were anyone else, this spineless Republican Party wouldn't have the guts to indict us, put us on trial, or hold us accountable."

But courage inspires courage. And Donald Trump exudes both.

If anyone is going to bring these corrupt jackals to justice, it will be President Trump in his second term. Justice will come for them—with a force they've never seen—and it will shatter their corrupt lives.

I believe these were the thoughts of fear bouncing around in their minds—like vampires afraid of the rising sun.

Courage or cowardice—both have a cost. It's just a matter of what you're willing to pay, and who you really are.

Ultimately, words don't matter. It's what we do—or don't do—that truly defines us.

This blind, irrational hatred of Donald Trump—so intense it overrides even love of country—is nothing short of insanity. The thousands of lives lost under the Biden administration don't even account for the future terrorist attacks that many experts say are inevitable. FBI personnel have testified before Congress that open borders pose a real and growing threat. With thousands of potential terrorists infiltrating the country, it's not a matter of *if*—but *when*.

And when that moment comes, those killers won't be asking who's a Democrat or Republican. Even those suffering from Trump Derangement Syndrome or Democrat brainwashing are putting themselves and their loved ones in danger. The fact that they're willing to risk national security and personal safety raises a chilling question: what else are they willing to do?

Given everything they've already tried—fake investigations, the raid on Trump's home at Mar-a-Lago, and lawfare designed to imprison him—it's hard not to wonder if they've crossed so far past the point of no return that the only thing left was assassination.

Those who orchestrated the 2020 fraud election and enabled years of open borders clearly had no issue exposing America to danger. Would they really balk at the idea of eliminating a political threat?

Much like everything else done on behalf of the Democrat Party, there have been no real consequences. The would-be assassins would be disposable. The Justice Department and mainstream media would remain compliant. Republicans would do what they always do—raise their voices, then roll over.

The outrage from Trump supporters would be massive, perhaps even violent. But eventually, cooler heads would prevail. Why? Because at its core, the Republican Party is one of higher principles—always preferring the high road. Whether that's courage or cowardice is debatable.

Let's be honest: the United States wasn't founded by taking the high road. It was founded through necessary violence—the American Revolution. If someone breaks into your home or threatens your family, violence may very well be the answer. World history is filled with wars that began when reason failed. If the Founders had embraced a "violence is never the answer" mindset, there would be no America.

There are real questions that need to be asked. Anyone paying attention knows Joe Biden is incompetent and being led by handlers. Endless videos show him shaking hands with thin air, calling on deceased individuals to speak, falling downstairs, falling off a bicycle, and attending press conferences with preselected reporters and scripted questions.

So who was really making decisions in the White House?

Many believe it was President Obama, George Soros, China—or some combination of them. What was expected of Joe Biden in exchange for the millions of dollars funneled to Hunter Biden from China, Ukraine, and Russia, as revealed in congressional investigations? What did he agree to do—or ignore?

Why was a Chinese "weather balloon" allowed to fly across the entire country, even hovering over military sites?

In a very real sense, Joe Biden may be the first Manchurian candidate in American history.

Trump's third presidential campaign posed a serious threat to all of them. If they were willing to run a fraudulent election in 2020 and threaten Trump with 700 years in prison through lawfare, how much further would they go? Could they have been planning the unthinkable?

President Lincoln is a tragic example that such things *can* happen.

These are serious questions—and we may never get the answers. There's an old saying: true power rests behind the throne. Whoever was truly running America had all the power of the presidency—and none of the responsibility.

In the bigger picture, Joe Biden was never the "Big Guy," as described in Hunter Biden's communications. He was the fall guy—the one who would take the blame, the shame, and any criminal charges. And if pressed, he'd simply say he couldn't remember.

In a sense, this could be considered the perfect crime. They could do anything—without consequences.

Even amid the corrupt lawfare, there were already concerns about Trump's safety. Rumors of assassination circulated. Many demanded Trump receive extra security. And rightly so.

We had every reason to be concerned about the mountain of corruption within the FBI, CIA, DOJ, and the rest of the deep state. These agencies weren't acting independently. Every mountain has a peak—so who was sanctioning these investigations and operations?

As mentioned before, many believe it was President Obama or members of his staff. If Trump won, his Attorney

General and others would dig into the corruption and take action.

James Comey, John Brennan, and others aren't going to serve 10 to 20 years for anyone. When push comes to shove, they'll talk.

Obama, Biden, and the rest will have a lot of explaining to do—and may very well face criminal charges.

The point is this: if Trump doesn't win—or if something tragic happens to him—all of this will simply disappear.

And as any law enforcement detective will tell you: they had plenty of motive for that outcome.

As President Trump's third run for office continued, we could all feel it building toward something monumental. They had gone after him, his friends, and his inner circle with one ridiculous investigation after another. Those close to him were charged, held in contempt, or sentenced to jail time. Peter Navarro and Steve Bannon are two examples of individuals in Trump's orbit who refused to cower before the corrupt Biden administration.

Trump himself was found guilty of 34 so-called felonies—charges the Democrats and the mainstream media repeated ad nauseam. Most people not paying close attention didn't realize these were originally misdemeanors, with expired statutes of limitations. At worst, they would have resulted in a fine—similar to the one Hillary Clinton paid. Of course, no charges were brought against her, and her home was never raided like Trump's.

The media failed to explain that Alvin Bragg, as Assistant District Attorney, had previously declined to bring these charges, stating there was nothing there. Others in the Justice Department refused as well. But in this new era of lawfare under the Biden administration, legal gymnastics were used to turn misdemeanors into felonies.

The so-called 34 felonies were actually accounting entries related to payments to Stormy Daniels. If one check had been sent, it would have amounted to one charge. Instead, they split it into dozens. This was a travesty of justice, and any decent appeals court should overturn it.

Once again, the mainstream media worked their magic—pulling the wool over the eyes of half the country. It's masterful, the way they report information in a one-sided fashion, omit key details, or avoid reporting the story altogether. They've convinced millions that these investigations and lawsuits against President Trump are legitimate.

Meanwhile, Joe Biden possessed far more classified documents—many from his time in the Senate and as Vice President—with absolutely no legal authority to have them. These documents were unsecured, and the case should have been open-and-shut for any competent federal prosecutor. Yet half the country remains unaware of these facts, because the media refuses to lay them bare.

Those who rely on mainstream outlets like CNN or FM radio have little understanding of how these cases were built—or the lack of evidence behind them. The good news is that half of America *does* know the truth. They see the mainstream media for what it really is: an extension of the Democrat Party.

This comes as no surprise to anyone paying attention. Most mainstream journalists are Democrats. They socialize with Democrat politicians, form relationships, and share ideological views. But none of that should matter when it comes to their profession.

The media owes it to America to report both sides of every issue—fairly and without bias. If they can't do that, they're useless. Most of us who are paying attention know they haven't done this in a very long time.

It gives me no joy to say this. I remember a time when there were respect and reverence for the FBI, and for news outlets like ABC and NBC. Now, more than half of America doesn't trust these institutions—and for good reason. They've done this to themselves.

President Trump is not to blame. Republicans aren't to blame. People who disagree with their worldview aren't to blame. The fault lies solely with them. They've allowed politics and emotional hatred to override professionalism and integrity.

These traits—professionalism and integrity—must be guarded like money or gold. Because in a very real way, they *are* that valuable. Once lost, they're nearly impossible to regain. It's like a spouse who repeatedly cheats and destroys their family. Trust, once broken, is hard to rebuild.

Believe it or not, it's my sincere hope that these institutions can somehow restore the integrity they've destroyed. Whether you call it Trump Derangement Syndrome or Democrat brainwashing, they must confront this issue if they ever want to reclaim their credibility. If they can't, they should step aside and make room for those who can.

We need a mainstream media that acts as the policeman of truth—reporting both sides without bias. That means covering the good and bad from both parties. When one party goes off the rails, as the Democrat Party has, journalists should call it out from a place of integrity—without apology.

That should be the goal of any reporter who truly cares about their profession.

As it stands, the media can't criticize Republicans without looking like hypocrites—after all the disinformation and biased reporting they've done. They've dug themselves into a deep hole. And it's a steep hill they'll have to climb to get out of it.

I sincerely hope they can. Because if they can't, we need to take a hard look at whether these institutions should survive.

Many believe the FBI is so corrupt it's beyond saving—and there's plenty of evidence to support that view. Perhaps the mainstream media should face federal oversight or have their licenses revoked. There's growing support for that idea, too.

These are serious questions America will have to grapple with in the years ahead.

It's my belief—and my hope—that these institutions understand how despicable, corrupt, and often treasonous their behavior has been. If they don't grasp this to their core, they should no longer exist as we know them.

The FBI and other law enforcement agencies should be disbanded, with their duties reassigned to the U.S. Marshals and other trustworthy agencies. Media licenses should be suspended, evaluated, and regulated under a bipartisan oversight system—equally divided between Republicans and Democrats.

If this needs to be done, then it *must* be done. Simple as that.

America doesn't have time to play games with this issue. Serious corrections and consequences are needed—firings, indictments, prosecutions—whatever it takes to right the ship.

Do these actions seem cruel? Tell that to the parents of Angel families who buried loved ones because of the Biden administration's policies, the media's refusal to report the truth, and corrupt law enforcement agencies that either participated or stayed silent.

There are serious questions surrounding assassination attempts on President Trump—which we'll be addressing shortly.

They were the cruel ones.

And that must never be forgotten.

The point is—why was all of this happening?

Joe Biden was essentially stepping down after a disastrous debate performance. All of America saw firsthand that he was incompetent, likely had been for some time, and wasn't running anything that mattered. Incoherent, stumbling over his words, babbling—these were just some of the terms used, even by members of the mainstream media who had spent years making excuses for him.

The veil that the White House and media had pulled over half the country's eyes was finally coming off.

Even Jake Tapper of CNN, who had previously defended Biden and assured America he was fine, released a book titled *Original Sin*. The *New York Times* described it as "a damning portrait of an enfeebled Biden protected by his inner circle." Tapper admitted that he and the mainstream media failed to aggressively report on Biden's declining health during his presidency.

This is the same media that wants America to trust them about the 2020 election and a host of other issues concerning Trump.

Why this was a surprise to millions is a mystery to me— after years of Biden shaking hands with thin air, being guided off stage by the Easter Bunny, and other bizarre moments. Somehow, the media managed to explain it away to those willing to believe them.

After Biden insisted he was staying in the race, rumors resurfaced that the real power behind the White House was pressuring him to bow out. Soon after, Biden reappeared and gave a short speech announcing he was stepping aside. Vice President Harris would be stepping forward to run in his place.

I'm sure Democrat Party leaders thought she was a better candidate—and being a person of color certainly didn't hurt. What they fail to see is that none of this would be necessary if their platforms were solid and their policies made sense.

In the face of everything they've done, why is Donald Trump still so popular?

The truth is nothing they did was going to work. The four years of their administration were a nightmare for anyone paying attention. Even that wouldn't have mattered—because politically, Donald Trump is a force of nature. In any election even remotely fair, no Democrat was going to beat him.

Simply put, his policies made sense. He was the best man for the job. The American people knew it—and so did they.

I believe this realization left only one option in their minds. The unthinkable was on the table. Perhaps it had been there all along.

As I've written before, anyone paying attention to the Biden administration knew Joe wasn't running anything. Neither was Vice President Harris. The real decision-makers were names we all know well. I've mentioned a few already, but I doubt we'll ever know the full truth.

Some of you reading this might think, "That sounds too crazy. It could never happen. Our government is better than that." Unfortunately, we all know that's not the case. Perhaps it never was.

Newsweek recently reported that Biden's White House physician invoked his Fifth Amendment rights before a

House Oversight Committee—fueling accusations of a cover-up regarding Biden's declining mental health. The physician did this after being asked whether he was told or pressured to lie about Biden's condition.

Others in Biden's staff also took the Fifth before Congress.

The obvious question: why are all these people pleading the Fifth if everything was above board?

Americans are growing increasingly disgusted with this administration and wondering—when will these people be held accountable?

Perhaps the corrupt Democrat deep state was wondering the same. Perhaps they had come this far and decided they might as well go the rest of the way horrible as it sounds.

It's been decades since the assassination of JFK, and there are still valid questions that remain unanswered. They may never be answered—either because our government is incompetent and truly doesn't know, or worse, because they know exactly what happened and refuse to tell the public.

This mindset—that the public "can't handle the truth"—has existed throughout history. But that's beside the point. We are not a dictatorship. We are a free country, and we deserve to know the whole truth—the good, the bad, and the ugly.

They hide behind terms like "national security," "sources and methods," and other bureaucratic jargon designed to keep the truth secret. More often than not, it's to protect themselves from embarrassment or criminal exposure.

A second Trump administration would be terrifying for them—because if anyone could bring them to justice, it would be him.

Thomas Paine, the influential American revolutionary, once said:

"A body of men holding themselves accountable to nobody ought not to be trusted by anybody."

Some ideas are timeless.

We are living in a time when our national agencies—those entrusted with law enforcement, safety, international relations, and intelligence—have proven themselves to be trustworthy and unaccountable.

Congressional investigations have revealed everything from the fake Russia hoax to Biden family corruption involving money from foreign adversaries funneled through shell companies. Many of these individuals—FBI, CIA,

Biden family members—should be facing indictments, arrest warrants, and court appearances in jailhouse jumpsuits.

Instead, we see none of it.

If this were ordinary citizens, the outcome would be very different. Consider the Navy sailor who took classified photos on a nuclear submarine to impress his friends—he went to jail. These people have done far worse.

Americans have lost faith in their institutions—from state governors and Congress to the presidency itself. We've endured years of corruption, fake investigations, and FBI agents plotting against Trump—talking about "insurance policies," submitting false information to FISA courts, and launching investigations based on a dossier paid for by Hillary Clinton and the DNC.

This era under the Biden administration will go down as one of the darkest and most corrupt in American history.

The government itself became the criminal—ignoring the laws of the land, erasing guardrails, and twisting statutes to suit their agenda.

"Show me the man, and I'll show you the crime."

This quote, attributed to Soviet secret police chief Lavrentiy Beria, perfectly captures the mindset of the Biden Justice Department.

They started with the person—then went looking for a crime.

Americans were held in jail for three to four years without bail hearings for what amounted to trespassing and being belligerent with Capitol Police on January 6th. Most murderers, child molesters, and rapists are treated better.

But if you're a Trump supporter or conservative, equal justice doesn't apply.

The Biden administration's criminal and corrupt behavior had no shame—and no bottom.

This administration was capable of literally anything.

Anything.

July 13th, 2024, will go down as one of the worst days in modern American history—not only for the horrific act that occurred, but for the despicable reaction from many on the Democrat side. It was only by an act of God—or extraordinary luck—that President Trump was not killed that day.

At a rally in Butler, Pennsylvania, Trump had just taken the stage and begun his speech when the unthinkable happened: shots were fired at the President.

Here are the basic facts of that tragic day. The 20-year-old would-be assassin, Thomas Crooks, was killed on the rooftop. Though registered as a Republican—likely to vote in a closed primary—he had donated money to the Democrat Party and was from the nearby town of Bethel Park, Pennsylvania.

Local police noticed Crooks more than an hour before the shooting. He was seen surveying sniper positions and examining the stage through a gun range finder. At one point, Crooks ran from officers who were actively watching for him. He evaded police until he was later spotted on the roof.

A Butler Township police officer climbed a ladder to reach the rooftop. The officer later reported that after they locked eyes, Crooks pointed a rifle at him. The officer slipped and fell to the ground, yelling into his radio, "He's got a gun. He's got a long gun."

The task force investigating the assassination attempt has not received any evidence that this message reached Trump's Secret Service detail before shots were fired.

Crooks fired eight rounds, wounding President Trump and other supporters, and killing one brave man who shielded his family. A member of the Butler County Emergency Services Unit shot at Crooks and hit his rifle, preventing further shots. Ten seconds later, Crooks was shot and killed by the Secret Service.

You don't have to be in law enforcement to have serious questions about these events. If Crooks was spotted more than an hour before the shooting, were those details known to the Secret Service? Why wasn't Trump's appearance delayed until the situation was resolved? Why did the Secret Service wait until eight shots were fired—and ten seconds after another officer disabled Crooks' rifle—before taking the kill shot?

We may never know how much of this was incompetence—or something worse. All we're left with are empty excuses and denials from a government that has lost the public's trust. Remember, these are the same people who couldn't tell us whose cocaine was found in the Biden White House. "We may never know" was the official response to that so-called investigation.

The head of the Secret Service later resigned, and Congress began discussions about further investigations into the assassination attempt.

This was a tragic day that should never be forgotten—though the mainstream media will do its best to ensure that it is.

I feel deep pain and sorrow for the Trump supporter who died shielding his family. Thank God President Trump survived. Whether half of America realizes it or not—they need him.

I've always felt anger and empathy for crime victims. I don't have to know them personally. I just try to imagine being in their shoes at that moment. Our society has become too callous. Too often, we see a tragedy on television, shake our heads, and then go back to our routines.

But know this: somewhere out there, a real tragedy is unfolding. A family is living through their worst nightmare. They've lost a husband, wife, child—someone they deeply love. It's an emotional earthquake shaking their home to its core. And but for the grace of God, it could be any of us.

How can we not feel their pain?

Regardless of how you feel about Donald Trump, he is someone's husband, father, and friend. He is loved by his family. How can anyone not feel for them—or worse, make fun of it?

The behavior of many Democrats was truly despicable and unworthy of American citizens. They should have been ashamed—but most were not. Some claimed it was a hoax, designed to make Trump look better—even if it meant someone being shot or killed. Others joked that Trump deserved it or wished the gunman had better aim.

It didn't matter that people were wounded or that one brave man died protecting his family. Many of those making these comments weren't just random internet trolls—they were churchgoers, professionals, teachers. It didn't matter to them that Trump is an American and a human being. Their blind hatred was all that mattered. Many found the whole thing humorous.

What is wrong with these people?

That was—and still is—my reaction to the Democrat Party, of which I was once a member. If this had happened to President Obama, we all know what the reaction would have been: outrage, and rightly so. If it had happened to any Democrat, I would be outraged as well. Whether you agree with someone politically or not, no one deserves that.

But when it comes to Trump, none of it matters to them. Only their hatred.

It's deeply sad when emotion overrides someone's ability to think clearly. The worst part is—they don't even realize it. There's truth to the idea that crazy people don't know they're crazy.

I once saw a crime show called *Evil Lives Here*. They interviewed a convicted rapist and murderer who had killed at least seven women. He became upset when he saw the title—because he didn't see himself as "evil." I imagine many murderers, child molesters, and criminals feel the same way.

In many aspects, this is the Democrat Party.

And incredibly, there was a second attempted assassination of President Trump.

On September 15, 2024, President Trump survived a second assassination attempt—an event that not only shocked the nation but exposed the deep moral divide in American political culture.

At Trump International Golf Club in West Palm Beach, Florida, 58-year-old Ryan Routh was discovered hiding in shrubbery, aiming a rifle at a member of Trump's security detail. A Secret Service agent spotted the barrel of the weapon and opened fire. Routh fled the scene and was later apprehended in Martin County. Thankfully, no injuries were reported, but officials confirmed that Routh had intended to assassinate President Trump. He had arrived the night before, concealed himself in the bushes, and waited for Trump to appear—positioned just 300 to 500 yards away.

This raises serious questions:

How did Routh know Trump would be there?

Why wasn't the golf course secured?

Why wasn't the threat detected earlier?

The brave agent who spotted the rifle may have prevented a national tragedy. But the fact that Routh was able to flee and drive away before being captured is deeply troubling. And once again, the reaction from many on the Democrat side was "despicable." Just like after the Butler, PA rally shooting, millions expressed disappointment that the assassin failed. Some joked about the aim, others claimed

Trump brought it on himself, and many simply refused to show any sympathy.

These weren't just fringe radicals. Many were professionals—teachers, churchgoers, and neighbors. Somehow, the fact that Trump is a human being with a family who loves him never crosses their minds. Nor is the possibility that those who disagree with them might be right. I'd like to believe that someday they'll look back and feel shame for being okay with the idea of Trump being murdered. But I doubt most of them will ever see the light.

The American people deserve answers.

Why was this allowed to happen? Was anyone complicit—inside or outside of government? Decades after JFK's assassination, we still don't have the full truth. President Trump promised to declassify those records—more than any other president ever did. But the fact that Americans are kept in the dark is unacceptable. What are they afraid we'll find out? That they were complicit—or simply incompetent?

We must pray for our presidents, whether we voted for them or not. This is about preserving the institution of the presidency. If you claim to love this country, that should not be too much to ask.

Ultimately, it doesn't matter if you're a president or a private citizen. As an American, you have the absolute right to express your political views without fear of assault or murder. What happened to "we can agree to disagree"? Someone being wrong or misinformed doesn't justify violence.

The Fire of Truth, the title of this book, is more than symbolic. Stepping into this fire—into the realm of facts, evidence, and common sense that people don't want to hear—is real. And so are the consequences. Those who step into it are warriors. This is a battlefield of ideas and truth. Whether you're nationally known or not, the reality is the same for everyone who chooses to speak out.

If you are one of these patriots—of God and of America— know this: you are the brave heroes this country needs, whether it realizes it or not. This is a battle of good versus evil. And evil doesn't wear a uniform. Many who stand on its side don't even know they're doing so. They could be your coworkers, your neighbors, fellow churchgoers.

Some can be reached—with God, facts, and reason. Many cannot. They are lost in the ocean of misinformation, Trump Derangement Syndrome, or apathy. Regardless, we must defeat the mindset they stand on.

135

We must defeat this intolerance—the refusal to hear opposing views, the inability to argue and win on merit. This is the mindset that tells you $2 + 2 = 7$, and demands you agree—or else. That you must believe it, or stay silent. This is the language of tyrants and those who unknowingly serve them.

I end this chapter with the tragic assassination of Charlie Kirk, founder of Turning Point USA and a nationally known conservative activist. On September 10, 2025, while speaking at a university in Utah, Charlie was shot in the throat by a rooftop sniper. He was rushed for medical attention, but hours later, it was announced that Charlie Kirk had been assassinated.

Charlie was a decent man—polite, religious, kind. He spent his life respectfully engaging students on college campuses, offering a conservative perspective to those who had never heard it. He visited over 3,500 schools and universities, and even traveled internationally to share his message. Students were encouraged to challenge him, ask questions, and think critically.

Charlie had interviewed leaders from both parties. He was 31 years old, with a wife and two young children.

And still—they assassinated him.

Some said Trump was too bombastic, too rude, too controversial. So they tried to kill him. Charlie was the opposite—gentle, respectful, and open-minded. And they still killed him.

This is a tragic lesson: there is no middle ground with this Democrat Party. It is a godless party of evil. Those who stand with it either don't know—or don't care.

We must reach those we can. We must fix our corrupt election system. We must vote Republican and, God willing, keep the Democrat Party out of power forever.

Charlie Kirk touched more lives in his short time on Earth than many do in a lifetime. And when Republicans in Congress asked for a moment of silence, Democrats refused.

Let that sink in.

Doesn't it bother anyone to know they're on the same political side as people who can't take a moment of silence for a murdered man who left behind a wife and two children?

What does that say about them?

What does it say about those who vote for them?

These are questions they may never answer—and perhaps never want to.

Chapter 6 The Enemy Within

President Lincoln once warned that the greatest danger to our nation "must spring up amongst us—it cannot come from abroad." I believe that great men possess wisdom that transcends time. It's not just insight into the issues they face, but a deeper understanding of the people who must make the best decisions possible. These decisions aren't always black and white. More often, they fall into the complex shades of gray that define life itself.

Much like a judge in a courtroom, we must ask: Is the maximum sentence justified? Are there extenuating circumstances? What is just punishment? Whether you're a judge in a courtroom or at your kitchen table, the concept is the same. Without a North Star—without God, wisdom, and common sense—these decisions become nearly impossible. Worse, they can become dangerous.

That North Star is your moral compass. Others may define it differently, but for me, it's rooted in truth, faith, and reason.

One of the major problems with the Democrat Party is that many lack this compass. And those who do have one often find it pointing in the wrong direction. This happens when emotion overrides logic, reason, and wisdom. The rest are simply brainwashed, ignorant, or uninterested in what's happening around them. They're like someone who causes a fatal car accident because they're drunk, distracted by Facebook, or glued to their phone.

History is full of decent people who allowed terrible things to happen. It's part of the human condition—and something we must always be vigilant against.

The word "battle" is significant. The Bible speaks of a time when good will be called evil, and evil will be called good. In some ways, that's black and white. In others, it's not. I don't believe most people knowingly choose the side of evil. They see themselves as enlightened, woke, progressive, open-minded. And in many ways, they probably are decent people.

But moral confusion—those shades of gray—are what we're dealing with. What's the exact point where a lighter shade of gray becomes darker? That's the defining question.

None of us are perfect. We all fall short. All we can do is strive to be better human beings in God's eyes and make the world better for having been here.

Those on the side of evil are often confused. They may feel they mean well. They may believe they're being compassionate. But it's not just individuals—it's the authorities we elect to lead our cities, states, and country.

Take the idea of no-cash bail. On the surface, it sounds fair. Shouldn't people in jail have an easier path to freedom? What if it were us—wouldn't we want that option?

These questions sound reasonable to someone with a subjective moral compass. I'm sure the people who advocate for these policies are good people—married, with families, churchgoers. Some are everyday citizens. Others are elected officials.

But they don't see the consequences. They don't see that these ideas, while well-intentioned, can lead to tragedy.

Case in point: a Michigan man out on no-cash bond for three previous murder charges was arrested again—this time for allegedly committing a fourth murder. There are countless examples like this involving rape, assault, and other violent crimes.

These victims had a right to live. A right to be protected. A right to expect that the officials they elected would look out for them.

This liberal-minded way of thinking is just as responsible for these crimes as the criminals who committed them. Judges, mayors, governors should be held criminally or financially liable. But they won't be. And it will happen again.

This isn't just incompetence. It's evil committed by decent people who mean well but do terrible things.

Releasing repeat offenders on no-cash bonds is evil. It's dangerous nonsense. And it happens when people lack a moral compass that points true north.

This Democrat mindset extends to open borders, gender-affirming surgeries for minors, and boys sharing locker rooms with girls. Don't be afraid to be called old-fashioned, a bigot, or a racist. These labels are meant to shame you into silence.

But this is a battlefield—of good and evil people, of good and evil ideas.

Those who promote these ideas don't walk around with horns and pitchforks. They're well-dressed. They work with us. They sit in church. They're our neighbors.

Make no mistake: this battle is real. And so are the consequences.

But for the grace of God, one of these victims could be your child, your spouse, your loved one. The victims you just read about were loved deeply. Their families are living through unimaginable pain.

Stand up—for God, for conservative principles, for common sense.

We owe it to ourselves—and to these victims—not to back down. Make the case to vote Republican. Speak up on social media, in your church, at the barber shop—anywhere people will listen. Be respectful, but be firm. Let them know this is about the victims suffering because of what others believe and vote for.

Many are too far gone. But some can be reached. Even if it's just 10% or 20%, that's progress. And we should embrace it.

The battle between good and evil has raged since the beginning of mankind. We are on the side of God, truth, and common sense.

Never forget that.

The danger from within is just as real today as it was in President Lincoln's time. One could argue it's even worse now, given our greater capacity for destruction and the limitless ignorance that seems to permeate our society. The Democrat Party was the enemy from within that Lincoln faced—it was the party of slavery, the party that fought a civil war to preserve it. The horrors of that era—lynchings, rape, the selling of families and children—were committed at their hands.

That legacy was followed by Jim Crow laws and, later, the welfare system that devastated generations. Today, they are the party of high crime in major cities, failing education systems, fraudulent elections, and corruption in institutions like the FBI, DOJ, and mainstream media. They are the party of misinformation, chaos, and confusion. They often side with criminals—defending them, speaking on their behalf—while ignoring the victims.

I'm particularly disappointed in law enforcement. Many conservatives say 99% of officers are good, and only 1% are corrupt. But I say to that 99%: if you participate in corruption, or stand by silently, there is no difference between you and the neighborhood thug taking orders from his gang leader.

Some say FBI and DOJ agents do what they must to protect their jobs. That excuse has echoed throughout history— from gang members to Nazi prison guards who led Jews to gas chambers. I'm sure many of them had families and bills, too. But long before they were law enforcement officers, they were American citizens and human beings—with the ability to know right from wrong in their souls.

When you retire, you return to being a citizen. And when you stand before the Almighty on Judgment Day, you will stand as a human being—not as a badge or a title. You won't be able to hide behind your profession.

Martin Luther King Jr. once said:

"The ultimate measure of a man is not where he stands in moments of comfort and convenience, but where he stands at times of challenge and controversy."

That statement is timeless. Standing up for truth and justice always comes with a cost—which is why so many avoid it. Any law enforcement or military veteran will tell you: those who go through the door first, or over the hill, take the most punishment. Being the point of the spear—whether in battle or in the fight for truth—always comes with a price.

There will always be justifications for doing evil. That's the mindset of the Democrat Party: chaos, death, corruption, and destruction—wrapped in nonsense explanations.

Wherever they go, ruin follows. Like locusts, they stay until a place is drained of value, then move on.

We see this when people flee Democrat-run cities and states—only to bring their failed policies to red states. If Democrat ideas were so great, everyone would be moving to places like New York, Chicago, and San Francisco. But they're not.

Instead, they come to red states and impose their will—through lawfare, crime, fraudulent elections, and name-calling. They'll call you a "racist" just to put you on the defensive.

Colorado is a prime example—a red state led into ruin and submission, now blue. On a larger scale, this is the lesson of open borders. When your city or state is overrun, it becomes unrecognizable. France, Germany, England—unless they take a stand, they will soon no longer be the majority in their own countries.

It's a hard truth: some people cannot be reasoned with. Many are leaders of populations that either don't know or don't care. Trying to accommodate them or find middle ground is a waste of time. Their idea of compromising is calling you names and getting everything they want—until they come back for more.

Case in point: Fox News recently reported that ICE and other federal law enforcement officers were ambushed in Texas. The Justice Department named ten individuals charged with shooting a police officer in the neck and opening fire on correctional officers outside the Prairieland Detention Center in Alvarado, Texas.

Ten minutes after gathering at the ICE facility, one or two individuals broke off and began spray-painting vehicles with phrases like "ICE pig." When correction officers called 911, an Alvarado police officer responded. As he exited his vehicle, one defendant—positioned in nearby woods—allegedly shot him in the neck. Another attacker fired 20 to 30 rounds at unarmed correction officers.

The shooting was captured on CCTV and the officer's body camera. The group fled separately. They were dressed in black military-style clothing, some wearing body armor and carrying two-way radios. Law enforcement found 12 sets of body armor, spray paint, ammunition magazines, and flyers reading "Fight ICE terror with class war."

Shortly after, another attack occurred. A man in a utility vest, armed with an assault rifle, fired dozens of rounds at federal agents and a U.S. Border Patrol facility in McAllen, Texas.

It's a miracle no law enforcement officers were killed.

I wonder—does it bother Democrats to know they're politically aligned with people like this? Do they even care?

Do these sound like people who can be reasoned with?

Republicans—and any decent Americans—need to wake up, smell the coffee, and realize exactly who we're dealing with.

They must be confronted—firmly, lawfully, and without apology. Policies must be enforced, and new laws or guidelines voted in if necessary. Whether they realize it or not, these are the steps Colorado and parts of Europe should have taken. They were in a struggle for their states and countries as they once knew them. If they want to see their future, they need only look at New York, Chicago, San Francisco—cities plagued by crime, mismanagement, and crushing taxes.

This is the true struggle for America as well.

It is dangerous for the Republican Party—and for any freedom-loving American—not to recognize the threat for what it truly is. Confrontation is a natural part of life. Those who refuse to stand up for themselves will be seen as weak and will invite trouble, whether they realize it or not.

A logically thinking person who deals in reality knows you must be ready for trouble—even when you don't want it. Practice for confrontation the same way you would for a golf swing, a tennis backhand, or a basketball jump shot. Whether it's a battle of ideas or a physical defense, preparation matters. This isn't just political advice—it's life advice. Those who come looking for trouble will always have a problem with someone who's ready for it.

Those who walk through life hoping to avoid confrontation set themselves up to be victims. They will be seen as naïve or weak-minded fools. Because at their core, the Democrat Party and those who think like them are tyrants. That's what they've always been. They are the enemy within.

They've also become masters of brainwashing— convincing millions of Democrats to forget their own history. Imagine a political party that ran slavery, fought a civil war to preserve it, opposed the 13th and 15th Amendments, and enforced Jim Crow laws. Then, years later, they convince Black Americans to vote for them 90–95% of the time. That's not just manipulation—it's masterful deception.

The insidious nature of brainwashing is that you walk around thinking everything is fine—and that everyone else is the problem. Why can't people understand that if a man believes he's a woman, he should be allowed to compete in women's sports, win awards, and be celebrated? That a 13-year-old girl who believes she's a boy should be allowed to undergo surgery and take medication? That open borders—despite the disease, crime, terrorism, and higher taxes—should be embraced, and illegal immigrants should vote in our elections?

Why is it acceptable to weaponize the justice system, raid President Trump's home for documents—a move unprecedented in American history—while ignoring the fact that President Biden had more documents, in more places, unsecured and taken from SCIFs during his time in the Senate and as Vice President?

That's a clear violation of the Espionage Act.

Yet Special Counsel Robert Hur refused to prosecute Biden, claiming he was "an elderly man with a poor memory." So we're supposed to believe Biden is too incompetent to stand trial—but competent enough to be president and run for a second term?

They see nothing wrong with any of this. But if it had happened to President Obama or Hillary Clinton, they'd be outraged—and rightly so.

These examples are bricks being pulled from the foundation of our country. And like any building, at a certain point, it collapses under its own weight. That's been the fate of many historic cities and nations. It's a lesson from history we must stop repeating.

I pray this is not the destiny of this great country we call America.

If history is told truthfully, the Biden administration will go down as one of the most treasonous, corrupt, and incompetent in American history. From Joe Biden and his son allegedly taking bribes from China, Ukraine, and Russia, to corrupt lawfare and open borders exposing us to countless dangers.

Open borders are perhaps the most dangerous of all.

Let's take the 10 million illegal immigrants the Biden administration admits have entered the country. The real number is likely double. Even if only 1% are terrorists, that's 100,000 jihad-minded individuals roaming freely. For perspective—9/11 was carried out by just 19.

And these numbers are conservative.

The Biden administration behaved like a thief in a stolen car—and the Democrat Party is responsible for immense damage. High crime rates, failing education, sky-high taxes. Every weekend, we hear about drive-by shootings, murders, rapes, assaults—all in Democrat-run cities.

Many of these so-called "riots" have been exposed as organized and funded. Videos show pallets of bricks delivered to protest sites. Ads on Craigslist offered $6,500 per week for "tough bad asses" in Los Angeles—with no clear job description. Witnesses reported buses arriving at protest rallies that quickly devolved into violence.

Add to this the fake Russia investigations, fraudulent elections, corrupt lawfare, and FBI agents discussing "insurance policies" to stop President Trump.

Ultimately, the greatest threat to America is not China or Russia—it's the Democrat Party from within. They will destroy us from the inside and aid our enemies on the outside.

To their credit, Democrats stick together. They vote in lockstep. They risk their reputations, even their careers, to support lies and disinformation. Republicans, meanwhile, have truth, evidence, and common sense—but they are timid.

The Republican Party is not perfect. But they are far better than the alternative.

Still, they've failed America by doing too little. They are the embodiment of good men doing nothing while evil thrives.

Who is worse—the thief who steals your car, or the policeman who watches and does nothing? The district attorney who refuses to prosecute? The judge who won't hear the case? The reporter who won't tell the story?

A strong argument can be made that it's not the thief. He's just being a criminal. The institutions that allow him to continue are the greater danger.

These are the people we rely on for protection, justice, and truth. When society loses faith in its institutions, it's a dangerous moment.

Why listen to mainstream media that can't report without bias? Why trust law enforcement or judges when the law doesn't apply equally?

When those who commit serious crimes walk free, while others face harsh punishment for far less—what does that say?

President Trump and his allies—Roger Stone, General Flynn, Peter Navarro, and others—are the definition of this two-tiered justice system. Meanwhile, Joe Biden pardons his family, and Democrats go on to work for CNN and MSNBC.

That's why institutional integrity matters. Once lost, it's nearly impossible to regain.

They must remember they govern by our consent.

As American citizens, we have the absolute right to verified elections, a fair justice system, and an unbiased media. We have the right not to be endangered by open borders.

Consent can be given—and it can be taken away.

When government loses that moral and legal authority, it becomes nothing more than jackbooted thugs in uniform.

Words once considered "crazy talk"—revolution, civil war, secession—become dangerously real.

History has shown this time and again. America itself was born from revolution. And our capacity for destruction is far greater now.

No one wants to walk down that road.

This is a battle to save America as we know it—from the enemy within. It's not some distant conflict that may happen in the future. This battle is here and now. There is no cavalry coming over the hill to rescue us—because the cavalry is us.

The Democrat Party has become lawless and corrupt. Many Democrats either don't know what their party has become—or don't want to know. The rest simply don't care. That's why they run fraudulent investigations, rig elections, arrest anyone in Trump's orbit, and even force attorneys to testify against their own clients. Attorney-client privilege is one of the cornerstones of our legal system, yet even that doesn't stop this corrupt party when they're targeting Trump.

They behave this way because they know they can count on Republicans to complain loudly—and then roll over. The Republican Party still doesn't truly understand who they're dealing with. Democrats don't care if we take the high road, turn the other cheek, or try to bridge the gap. They don't care how many chances we give them. Ethics, morals, integrity, religion—these are concepts they discard when it suits their purpose.

For them, the ends justify the means—even when the ends are wrong.

At their core, the Democrat Party are tyrants. To them, compromise means seeing things their way and getting what they want. Believe, think, and vote as they do—or else. That's who they are. The only thing they truly understand and respect is consequences and punishment. If we want to stop lawfare, fraudulent elections, sanctuary city policies, and everything else they're doing wrong, that's what it will take. Anything less is a waste of time.

Courage is what it will take to save this country—and perhaps even the world.

"The truth will set you free." That quote from John 8:32 is more than spiritual—it's practical. Jesus told a group of believers that if they remained faithful to his teachings, they would be set free. I believe people can be freed physically—and mentally. Truth can be beautiful, inspiring, and liberating. But it can also be harsh, shocking, and uncomfortable.

The Fire of Truth

What I've written about the Democrat Party is a harsh truth. There are decent Democrats, low-information voters, those suffering from Trump Derangement Syndrome, and others who are simply brainwashed. They're the passengers in the truck that's trying to run you over. Some want to be there. Some don't care. Some sense something is wrong but are too afraid to speak up. The driver, of course, is the corrupt and lawless Democrat Party.

It takes courage to admit you've been wrong for a long time. Many don't have that courage. It's easier to go along with the crowd. But "the truth will set you free" doesn't mean it's easy. It means it's possible—if you have faith and courage.

Those of us who've made that journey can tell you: it's tough. But there's no substitute for thinking clearly. Once you become a free thinker, there's no going back.

"Ignorance is bliss" carries truth as well. Ignorance simply means a lack of knowledge—it's not an insult. We're all ignorant of something. Most of us don't know how to fly a 747, and that's okay. As children, we were happiest because we didn't know—and didn't want to know.

In many ways, which describes much of the Democrat Party when confronted with objective facts.

Are open borders great for the country? Would anyone reading this allow ten complete strangers to move into their home indefinitely?

Defunding the police will reduce crime? Thousands of men, women, and children murdered and assaulted in our cities every year prove otherwise.

America is a racist country. As a Black man, I'll tell you: yes, racism exists. But so does dust in your home. If you look hard enough, you'll find it. The point is—it doesn't stop you from chasing your dreams.

America isn't perfect. But there's no better place in the world for Black people. No other country has as many Black millionaires. Our biggest obstacle isn't the white man—it's ourselves. If you're harmed as a person of color, odds are the perpetrator will look like you.

I wish Black lives mattered more to Black people.

We entertain nonsense ideas like "white people are the reason for all our problems." These are hard facts. But most Democrats don't know—and don't want to know. That's why they vote for the worst people to run their states and this country. Just look at the governors of California and New York—running their states into the ground.

Many of these people are simply grown-up children.

Once again, God-given, battle-tested common sense must be our moral compass. We must stop entertaining the nonsense of political correctness. It's not harmless. It's not a joke. It's a mindset that has put this country—and many others—in serious danger. It has already cost thousands of lives and could cost many more.

Sanctuary cities. Hiring based on race instead of ability. Releasing criminals with 30 or 40 arrests to harm innocent people. These are just a few examples of this dangerous mindset.

We cannot depend on weak politicians to fix it. They must be forced—or voted out.

The mainstream media, talk shows, and other outlets must hear the voice of common sense—regularly and without apology. Like an army trying to save a country that doesn't even know it's in danger, it is our duty to act anyway.

With the help of God, the American people, America First policies, and common sense—we pray we can succeed.

Because the alternative would be a nightmare.

Chapter 7 The Reckoning

The 2024 presidential election was upon us. Despite corrupt lawfare and assassination attempts, Donald Trump was more popular than ever. Why? Because most logically thinking, fair-minded people still have a basic sense of right and wrong. The biased coverage from the mainstream media, along with everything else thrown at him, may have actually helped elevate Trump into one of the most popular political figures in American history.

I've attended several Trump rallies, and the atmosphere is overwhelmingly positive. People are excited, hopeful, and genuinely want the best for our country. Attendees come from every age group, race, and nationality. They're polite, helpful, and respectful to one another. It's the kind of America I wish we could see more often.

It's hard to describe, but being at a Trump rally feels like being in an ocean of smiling faces—full of energy, laughter, and unity. I was fortunate enough to sit directly behind Trump at a rally in Georgia. His speeches have an authentic realness. He smiles, laughs, and connects with the crowd. I've heard a lifetime of political speeches like most of you have, and none of them come close. Some may disagree, but he's one of the best speakers I've ever seen.

As the speech ended and Trump waved to the crowd, I pointed him out to someone nearby. For some reason, he saw it—and pointed back directly at me. In a crowd of thousands, that moment felt personal. It may seem trivial to some, but it meant something. Those of us who are true Trump supporters understand that feeling. Caring about your fellow human beings is one of the highest forms of decency. And that, I believe, is who Trump is at his core—a good, imperfect man trying to do great things for this country we call America.

Donald Trump will go down as one of the most loved, controversial, and hated figures in American history.

There is very little middle ground with Trump. You either love him or hate him. As I write this, I do so with the full understanding that Trump is not everyone's cup of coffee. But we must never let personality or emotion guide our decision-making. We must rise above our feelings if we're going to make the best choices for our country.

This is very much a battle between good and evil. Where you stand defines the kind of person you are—and how much you truly care about others. It's not as black and white as it seems. Millions of decent Americans simply don't know what side they're truly on. Trump Derangement Syndrome, Democrat brainwashing, political correctness— these forces cloud their judgment.

It's like walking through a fog, unsure of where you are.

That's why having a moral compass is essential—for every human being, and especially for America, a global leader. Whether it's the Bible, God-given battle-tested common sense, or just a basic understanding of fairness, we need a North Star of truth to guide us.

Those who lack this compass are vulnerable to believing in nonsense. They're easily misled and may find themselves on the side of evil without even realizing it. That's what makes Trump Derangement Syndrome and political brainwashing so dangerous—their reach is limitless.

Those affected come from all walks of life. The smartest person in the room or the least informed. The oldest to the youngest. Black, white, rich, poor. From high-level executives to the guy who details your car. Without a North Star of truth, anyone can be lost.

I used to believe that logically thinking people could set aside emotion and look at problems objectively. Eventually,

I had to accept the sad truth: there aren't nearly as many logically thinking people as I thought. Many struggle to separate their feelings from facts.

When I debate these individuals, I sometimes make a list of issues and ask them to answer yes or no. Open borders allowing murderers, child molesters, rapists, and terrorists into our country. Sanctuary cities protecting criminal illegals. Men and boys competing in female sports. Dangerous repeat offenders released due to no-bail policies.

They say they're against these things. Then I ask: why do you vote Democrat? These are all Democrat policies. They tell me they're not for those things—but they vote Democrat anyway.

I tell them: you can't vote Democrat and claim you're not for these policies. You're putting the people in power who implement them—or do nothing to stop them.

At that point, I usually get loud, incoherent responses—and they walk away.

The truth is, they're on the side of horrible ideas and policies. To put it plainly, they're on the side of evil.

I've heard it said that evil isn't dark—it's bright like the sun. Many simply can't face it. If that's true, it may explain why they walk away, not realizing who they've aligned themselves with.

This, in a nutshell, is the conservative struggle: to bring our Democrat family and friends into the fire of truth.

Simply put, I will accept every awful thing you have to say about Donald Trump—the mean tweets, the bombastic behavior, the poorly worded statements. I accept it all. And I will vote for him anyway, because I know the number of good things he's done for the people of this country far exceeds his shortcomings.

I cannot say the same about the Democrat Party and its leaders. The amount of death, damage, and destruction they've brought to America far outweighs anything good they've ever done. I say this as someone who used to be a Democrat. It's painful to see the light of truth after being blinded by ignorance and nonsense for so long.

The real pain is for those who never see it—those we love who refuse to look, who don't want to know. Once you've seen the truth, you can never go back to not knowing, no matter how much your friends, family, or coworkers pressure you, threaten you, or plead with you.

There's a kind of closeness that's lost—a subtle disrespect that creeps in. They feel entitled to say things about your beliefs, to insult Trump or Republicans and expect you to excuse it. Any discussion or debate usually ends with them getting loud and shutting it down—after they've had their say, of course.

If you're a conservative, you're expected to sit down, shut up, and say nothing. Whether you're at the family dinner table or sitting in church, Democrats are allowed to pontificate with any nonsense they choose—without challenge or shame. Republicans are expected to take a deep breath, smile, and keep the peace. Apparently, that's our role—because we're the grown-ups in the room.

Meanwhile, Democrats feel free to get in the faces of Republicans at restaurants, movie theaters, and grocery stores—cursing them out, spitting on them, and behaving like immature, spoiled children. They post insulting, outrageous opinions on social media and get away with it. The so-called "fact checkers" almost always agree with the Democrat point of view. And of course, they're rarely censored or punished.

Let me repeat something that absolutely bears repeating:

When what you believe cannot stand up to disagreement, it's probably wrong.

When someone has to shout over you, interrupt you, or shut you down, it's usually because they know their argument is weak. Think about it—when someone truly knows they're right, why not let the other person speak?

If someone wants to explain to me that $3 + 3 = 8$, I'll give them a few minutes of uninterrupted time while I watch in disbelief.

These behaviors are rarely seen from the Republican side—because there's no need for them. We believe everyone has the right to speak their mind, whether they're right or wrong. That's not the Democrat mindset. Their tools are cancel culture, Facebook jail, suspended Twitter accounts, lawsuits, and threats—not better ideas or coherent arguments.

This is the philosophy of tyrants and dictators. These are the actions they take before resorting to brute force, national emergencies, or whatever term they choose to justify their power grabs.

The Democrat Party operates on an "or else" mindset.

Think the way they do. Vote the way they like. Don't object to their ideas or else.

The consequences are clear when you look at Donald Trump and those around him. Roger Stone, Peter Navarro, Mike Lindell—they've lived it firsthand. What they've been put through resembles the tactics of a dictatorship or a third-world regime.

This is why it's dangerous for any ordinary person to walk around a college campus or inner city wearing a MAGA hat or Trump gear. Doing so puts you at risk of being physically assaulted—or worse.

There have been many cases where this has happened. Trump supporters have been attacked, harassed, and even murdered. Attacks of this nature coming from the Republican side are extremely rare—if they happen at all.

Even after enduring the fake Russia investigation, two impeachments, the harassment and arrest of many in his inner circle, a corrupt and biased mainstream media, dishonest lawfare backed by the White House, kangaroo courts, and two assassination attempts—Donald Trump emerged as the Republican candidate for the 2024 presidential election.

Courage and grit are the only words that can describe what America—and the world—had the honor to witness. Many of us believe that only Donald Trump could have weathered this storm, financially, morally, and spiritually. Anyone else would have quit and run for the hills long ago.

In spite of all this—or perhaps because of it—Trump became a political force of nature unlike anything the world has ever seen. It has been both an honor and an outrage to watch it all unfold before our eyes. The sad part is that roughly half the country will never know the truth, blinded by irrational hatred and misinformation from the mainstream media.

The 2024 election was a phenomenon to behold. Trump rallies continued to draw massive crowds. Then came the debate—where Joe Biden revealed to the world what many of us had known since the beginning of his so-called presidency: that he was incompetent. The mainstream media knew it too, and they should go down in history as a corrupt, biased, disinformation machine with no integrity or honor.

Shortly after the debate, reports surfaced that members of Congress and others pressured Biden into giving a speech announcing his withdrawal from the race. Vice President

Kamala Harris would take his place. It didn't matter that the public never had the opportunity to vote for her as the Democrat Party's presidential candidate. As usual, Democrats found ways to bend or ignore the rules—assisted by a compliant media.

Much like waving the statute of limitations so Democrat district attorneys could bring politically motivated lawsuits and claim 34 felony convictions, the legal gymnastics never end. And there's always the expectation that they'll never truly be held accountable.

In the months that followed, the Harris campaign traveled the country with a fawning media entourage, collecting donations and endorsements from Hollywood, rappers, and other entertainers. Another presidential debate loomed on the horizon.

I've never understood why the Republican Party continues to participate in debates hosted by biased mainstream media outlets—especially when they've been caught giving information to Democrat candidates they favor. Take the case of Hillary Clinton receiving debate questions from Donna Brazile, as reported by ABC and CBS News.

In a fair debate, there should be one Democrat and one Republican moderator—each asking questions. It should not be CNN or ABC moderators pretending to be neutral when nothing could be further from the truth.

The presidential debate between Trump and Vice President Harris was yet another example. Claims surfaced that ABC moderators only fact-checked Trump and essentially sided with Harris, turning it into a three-on-one debate. There were also allegations that Harris's earrings may have been some kind of hearing device to assist her during the debate.

Given the Democrat Party's long history of election manipulation and unfair debate tactics, these claims cannot be dismissed out of hand.

There were claims made by Vice President Kamala Harris about working at McDonald's during her youth—but for some reason, she never provided proof. Even when accused of lying, she didn't offer pictures, IRS records, or any other documentation. If her claim were true, it would have been a perfect opportunity to show Trump up. Yet she couldn't even name the basic location of her supposed employment.

I worked at McDonald's myself over 30 years ago, and I can still tell you the location and provide IRS documentation if needed. Why couldn't she? The most likely answer is simple: she was lying.

If Donald Trump had made that claim, the mainstream media would have demanded dates, cities, IRS records—microphones in his face until he either proved it or admitted he lied. But, as with so many other things, Democrat leaders are given a pass on their lies and questionable behavior.

Incredibly, Trump didn't let the hypocrisy slide. He made arrangements to work the drive-thru window at a McDonald's himself. The media had no choice but to cover it. When Joe Biden referred to Trump supporters as "garbage," Trump turned the insult into a campaign moment—dressing in a reflective vest and sitting in a garbage truck, asking, "Anybody like it?"

That vest caught on like wildfire. Trump supporters across the country began wearing them in solidarity. Just another example of why we've never seen—and may never see again— a presidential candidate like Donald Trump.

The 2024 presidential election was a resounding victory for Trump. He won 312 electoral votes to 226, with over 77 million votes and a win in the popular vote. He swept every swing state, making it one of the most significant presidential victories in American history.

What made it even more stunning was that it happened despite Oprah, Beyoncé, and other Hollywood celebrities campaigning for Vice President Harris. Despite millions of illegal immigrants voting in California and other places. Despite election results in several states that still don't add up or make sense.

The American people rose up and elected Donald Trump again—despite everything the corrupt and treasonous Democrat Party had done to him since he entered politics.

Even with this great victory, Trump should have won Congress with more members. There are still questions that need to be asked and answered. What happened to the 81 million votes Biden and Harris supposedly received in 2020? The obvious answer: they never existed.

Does anyone really believe Arizona voted for Trump but not Kari Lake for Senate? Or that Nevada voted for Trump but not Sam Brown? It's the same ballot—so why is it discrepancy?

Why does it take California, Arizona, Nevada, and other states weeks to count ballots, while Florida and others finish in a day or two? Why are people in California voting from addresses that are just intersections or shopping malls?

In Pennsylvania's Delaware County, three election officials pleaded guilty to election fraud—accused of registering nearly three dozen nonresidents and casting ballots for them to sway an election.

It's embarrassing that in this age of technology and scientific advancement, we still can't run fair, verifiable elections.

Government officials and so-called experts will always offer excuses. But I'll take the word of people like Mike Lindell every day of the week. His researchers say Republicans should have gained six more seats in the Senate and nine in the House—and I believe him.

Beyond any doubt, the 2024 election was a great victory for Donald Trump—and for America. The illegitimate Biden administration made a series of disastrous decisions that caused immense damage to our country. President Trump and the rest of us now face the monumental task of correcting this tidal wave of corruption and incompetence. It will not be easy.

One of President Trump's first actions was securing our open borders and beginning the process of identifying and deporting criminal illegal immigrants for public safety. There are endless stories of Americans being assaulted and murdered—Laken Riley being one of the most heartbreaking examples. A University of Georgia student, she was attacked, beaten, and murdered while jogging on campus by an illegal immigrant who entered the country under Biden's open border policies. President Trump signed a law in her name to help prevent such tragedies from happening again.

Surrounding himself with a strong team, President Trump set about making real changes. In his first 100 days, he accomplished more than any president in American history. But the road has been anything but smooth. The Democrat Party has a long line of liberal judges who use the law to block executive orders and obstruct necessary actions. Trump and the Republicans must also confront a broken Department of Justice, FBI, CIA, and other agencies corrupted by Trump Derangement Syndrome.

These institutions must be held accountable for the damage they've done—fraudulent elections, lawfare, politically motivated investigations, and the violation of constitutional rights. Many January 6 defendants have been held in jail for years without bail hearings. Some were not involved in violence and were let inside the Capitol by police. The individual known as the "QAnon Shaman" was seen laughing and conversing with Capitol Police, who allowed him into rooms. They could have escorted him out at any time—but chose not to. Yet he was sentenced to three years and five months.

There must be accountability for what the Democrat Party and its agencies have done. They've inflicted unnecessary pain and expense on those they politically disagree with—many of whom did little or nothing to deserve it.

A reckoning is coming.

The word "reckoning" refers to settling an account, being held responsible, or facing consequences. It's the word that comes to mind when I think of the damage the Democrat Party has done to this country. There are decent Democrats who simply don't know—or don't want to know—what their party has become. Or more accurately, what it has always been.

From the days of slavery to the present, the Democrat Party has left a trail of chaos, pain, and millions of unnecessary deaths. And the worst part is—there may be more to come. There are likely tens of thousands of jihadist terrorists in our country right now, planning God only knows what. The Biden administration allowed our nation to be invaded with open border policies, bringing in anywhere from 10 to 20 million people.

Their goal? To flood swing states with illegal immigrants who will vote Democrat—so they can win elections without cheating like they did in 2020. What they failed to consider is that when you open your doors to everyone, you get everyone. And when tragedy strikes, terrorists won't ask who's a Democrat or Republican. If you're there, you're a target.

The Democrats handed these people the proverbial baseball bat—and they'll use it against us. Worse still, most Democrats don't even realize it, blinded by their hatred of Trump.

When I've had these discussions, the common response is, "What does it matter? We have crime anyway." That's a silly argument. We all have bills—light, water, and rent. Should everyone on your side of town drop their bills off at your house? Of course not. It's another example of how Democrat talking points collapse under logical scrutiny.

It's the same with sanctuary cities, lawfare tactics, waiving statutes of limitations to target political opponents, and holding J6 defendants for years without bail. Washington, D.C. itself is one of the most corrupt and crime-ridden cities per capita in America. Its murder rate is reportedly several times higher than Chicago or Philadelphia.

In a bold move, President Trump initiated a short-term law enforcement takeover in Washington, D.C., with help from the National Guard and other agencies. His goal: to improve life for the city's residents—most of whom are Black and didn't vote for him.

Naturally, the mayor and other officials who presided over this crime wave were outraged, promising protests and lawsuits. But President Trump is doing more to protect the people of D.C. than the very leaders they elected.

This is a perfect example of Democrat brainwashing overpowering common sense.

White House officials proudly reported that in over a week, there were zero murders in Washington, D.C.—a city plagued by violence. Citizens took to social media to express how much safer they felt and to thank the President.

No matter the final outcome of this bold experiment, President Trump has shown he is willing to help people of any color live safer, better lives—while Democrat leaders offer nothing but empty speeches.

It is my hope—and my prayer—that my people will someday wake up from this Democratic mental prison and free themselves.

As I've said before, I am an independent—and yes, I voted for Barack Obama twice. I say this because I want you to know that I'm open-minded and committed to truth above emotion. Voting for President Obama doesn't mean I'll turn a blind eye to the corruption, treason, and revelations that have come to light since.

The so-called Russia investigation is transforming into what many now call "Obamagate"—and for valid reasons. The FBI, CIA, and other agencies have released hundreds of declassified documents verifying that Obama had knowledge of—and often approved—the corrupt and politically motivated actions taken by his administration to target Donald Trump. This was a coordinated effort to distract from Hillary Clinton's email and server scandal.

Many Black Americans are quick to respond with anger and outrage. But I always ask the basic question: does what's being said sound true? Is there anything to it?

Most of the mainstream media—and half of America—have been lied to and misled since 2016. More declassified documents, once thought buried forever, have now been released. Whistleblowers are coming forward, leaving little doubt. The Russia investigation, which lasted years and cost over $30 million, targeted individuals simply for being in Trump's orbit. And it was all based on lies—lies the Obama-Biden administration knew from the beginning.

These lies were strategically leaked to a compliant, liberal-biased mainstream media, which then amplified them to the American public. When the dust settles, this will go down as one of the greatest scandals in American history.

We'll explore some of the evidence, but I'll say this: much of it rings true to me. There's been so much corruption from the Obama-Biden administration that I find myself asking not *if* they did these things—but *why wouldn't** they? They've done practically everything else and faced no real consequences. Why wouldn't they do this too?

It's like a judge who sees the same repeat offender over and over—it's tempting to pass judgment quickly. But logic and reason must prevail.

Unlike the Russia investigation, which was built on hearsay and political theater, Obamagate is backed by hundreds of declassified documents, emails, text messages, former Hillary campaign staffers, and whistleblowers. Even *The New York Times* referred to the evidence as "dawning."

Attorney General Pam Bondi has directed federal prosecutors to launch a grand jury investigation into accusations that Obama officials manufactured intelligence about Russian interference in the 2016 election. This grand jury could issue subpoenas or indictments as part of a criminal probe into whether Democrat officials tried to smear Donald Trump by falsely alleging collusion with Russia.

Director of National Intelligence Tulsi Gabbard summed it up:

"Former President Barack Obama and his intelligence officials allegedly promoted a contrived narrative that Russia interfered in the 2016 election to help President Trump win—selling it to the American people as though it were true. It wasn't."

Many—including myself—believe this not only happened in 2016, but has implications for the 2020 election, the raid on Trump's Mar-a-Lago home, the lawfare against him, and even the assassination attempts. What were they really searching for in Trump's home? Was it all part of a larger effort to stop him and cover up this historic scandal?

These Democrat leaders, their agencies, and the mainstream media have allowed their hatred of Trump to override professionalism, judgment, and basic decency. That's why integrity matters—because once it's lost, it's nearly impossible to get back.

It's like a spouse or family member who lies and betrays you for years. When they're finally caught, they're not sorry for what they did—they're sorry they got caught. And once exposed, everything they've ever told you must be questioned.

Some believe the FBI and other agencies shouldn't survive this scandal. That they should be disbanded, with responsibilities reassigned to the U.S. Marshals and other trustworthy institutions. I believe the new people President Trump has appointed may be able to save these organizations—if they can be saved.

The mainstream media should also be restructured—or replaced entirely. New leadership with courage and integrity is needed. There aren't enough pages in this book to express my disgust with the so-called journalists and reporters who failed us. They were supposed to be the ones we could trust to tell the truth and present both sides fairly.

Instead, they failed miserably.

They weren't just fooled by the Democrat deep state—many were complicit in the deception. Even now, with hundreds of declassified documents, emails, and texts available, many are still making excuses, trying to downplay the severity of this corruption.

NewsBusters, part of the Media Research Center, analyzed coverage from ABC, NBC, and CBS. They found that these networks gave 1,000 times more coverage to the fake Russia investigation in 2016 than to the bombshell evidence released by Tulsi Gabbard.

They preferred to cover a fabricated story over hard evidence.

The real tragedy is that millions of Americans still trust these networks—watching them nightly without question. The power they must feel is staggering: to have half the country believe whatever story they tell about Trump or anyone else.

They put Trump's family, friends, and administration officials through hell over a fake, contrived story designed to cover for Hillary Clinton's email scandal. General Flynn, Roger Stone, Peter Navarro, and others had their lives turned upside down—some even sent to prison—over an investigation that should never have happened.

If there's going to be justice for these people—and countless others—it must begin with the Obamagate scandal.

The Democrat Party must be held responsible for the damage it has done to America—and for the future threats that are now inevitable. Many district attorneys and government officials need to be investigated, charged, jailed, and have their law licenses revoked. Accountability is not optional—it's essential.

It has already begun. The FBI has launched an investigation into New York District Attorney Letitia James, alleging mortgage fraud. She is accused of signing false documents, misrepresenting herself as her father's wife, and claiming her official residence was in Virginia while serving as New York's DA. She also allegedly misrepresented the number of apartments in a rental property she owns to secure lower interest rates and tax advantages. Ironically, these allegations mirror the bogus charges brought against Donald Trump for his business dealings.

Atlanta District Attorney Fani Willis has also faced multiple investigations, primarily related to the 2020 election interference case against Trump and others. A Georgia judge ordered her to pay over $54,000 in attorney's fees for violating the state's open records act. There are also serious questions surrounding her romantic involvement with special prosecutor Nathan Wade, and whether both gave false testimony about the timeline of their relationship—potentially lying under oath.

The FBI has also arrested a Milwaukee County Circuit Judge for allegedly helping a Mexican national escape from immigration agents at the courthouse. In another case, a former New Mexico judge and his wife were arrested on federal charges for harboring an illegal immigrant and tampering with evidence.

I hope these are just the beginning. The reality, however, is that what *should* happen doesn't always *does*. Some prosecutors may hesitate to bring charges in places like New York and Washington, D.C., simply because these cities are too corrupt. Their populations voted overwhelmingly for Democrats—over 90%—and the same jury pools that convicted Trump on nonsense charges are still in place.

Yes, government attorneys have a point. But there's a bigger issue at play: even if the jury is biased, the charges must still be brought. Criminal and civil. Witnesses must testify. Facts must be laid bare for all to see. A reckoning must come for those who can be held accountable. For the rest, we must shame them with the truth—if they're capable of shame at all.

In a perfect country—or a dictatorship—these people would be swiftly brought to justice. They wouldn't be able to hide behind statutes of limitations or corrupt courts. Many would be sent to prison for the rest of their lives, which is exactly what they deserve.

Their treasonous actions surrounding the 2020 fraudulent election and the decisions made by the Biden-Harris White House have cost millions of lives. Open borders. The Russia-Ukraine war. The October 7th attack on Israel. And countless future lives that may be lost due to the terrorists and criminals they allowed to invade our country.

America is not perfect. Nor is it a dictatorship. So we must pursue the best justice we can under the circumstances. As much as I hate to say it, that may be the best we can hope for. But it's far better than nothing.

Truth, like aspirin, can be bitter going down—but it's often the best medicine. Some of what I've written may seem harsh, but it's written out of love for this country and its people. That's what you do when you care—you fight to save what matters, not just shake your head and walk away.

We're all in the same boat called America. When the actions of some threaten to sink it for everyone, we have a duty to speak up and act. The Democrat Party has done terrible things to this country. It has caused millions of unnecessary deaths and put us in grave danger for the future.

The leaders of this party—and those who carry out their agenda—are to blame. Many Democrats don't know, or don't want to know, what they're truly part of. They're like people in a crowd, seeing and hearing things that feel wrong—but following anyway. It's easier to go along than to stand up and walk away.

History has seen this before. The Nazi Party and others used fear and brainwashing to keep people from questioning their actions. Saving someone from others is hard. But saving someone from themselves is even harder.

What happens when the person in the mirror is the one who needs saving?

How do you rescue someone from a terrible idea they believe is wonderful? Telling them they're wrong isn't enough. Critical thinking must be taught—starting in schools. It helps us gain perspective and make better decisions.

God, the Ten Commandments, and religion must be brought back into schools. They provide a foundation that protects us from emotional nonsense and government brainwashing—from Hollywood, celebrities, and the media.

When something contradicts common sense or faith, question it. Seek the other side of the argument. And if the other side makes more sense, don't be afraid to admit you were wrong and change course.

God gifted us with the greatest intelligence on this planet. We must use it—in our decisions, our actions, and our beliefs. This should be our North Star. If we follow it and apply critical thinking, it will never fail us.

I said at the beginning: if you want to help others, tell them the truth. That's what this book is about. Speaking truth comes from love and respect. Some people don't know the truth because it's easier to believe what's comfortable— even if it's not real.

Whether they want it or not, the truth must be spoken. Even if it falls on deaf ears, the effort must be made. Like throwing a rope to someone drowning—it's simply the right thing to do.

Truth isn't always pleasant. It's often a bitter pill. But this isn't a book of cruel criticism—it's a book of truth and love. If someone is headed down a destructive path— gangs, crime, drugs—telling them it's wrong and urging them to change is an act of love. Shrugging your shoulders and walking away is not.

I pray for this nation. I pray that Americans who are misled, misinformed, or brainwashed will see the light of truth. Because we really are in the same boat—and if it sinks, we all go down with it.

Conclusion: The Fire Still Burns

As I look back over the long and winding road that led to the writing of *The Fire of Truth*, I see more than politics—I see a people searching for clarity in an age of confusion. We are a nation of contrasts and convictions, divided at times beyond recognition, yet united by a shared desire for something real, something honest, something lasting.

There were moments when the divide between us seemed unbridgeable. Friends stopped speaking, families split over ideals, and faith in institutions faded. But the distance was not truly political—it was spiritual. The bridge we must rebuild is not between parties, but between the human heart and the truth itself. The challenge of our time is not to agree on everything, but to remember that honesty and compassion must never be sacrificed for comfort or control.

When Donald J. Trump entered the national stage, he disrupted more than a political system—he disrupted complacency. His rise was a shock to the established order, a call for attention from those who had long felt unheard. Whether admired or criticized, his presence forced America to confront uncomfortable realities. He made us question the narratives we had accepted and encouraged us to think, debate, and awaken. That, in itself, became a defining moment in the life of the nation.

In the years that followed, the reaction was fierce and unrelenting. What many came to call *Trump Derangement Syndrome* revealed a deeper issue—the loss of our ability to listen, to reason, and to disagree without destruction. The storm of anger that followed his presidency was not merely political; it was cultural. Yet even in that storm, I found hope. Because chaos often comes before change, and honest disagreement, though painful, can lead to growth if we face it with open minds.

The election of 2020 brought both tension and transformation. It tested the limits of trust and the strength of democracy itself. But even through division, I was reminded of something eternal: the people still hold the power. No matter who leads, the heart of the nation beats in its citizens—the ones who rise each morning, work, pray, and care for one another. In their quiet strength lies the true foundation of this country.

The rising anger of recent years has too often turned violent, and the very thought of harm toward another human being over politics should give us pause. Those moments remind me that our greatest struggle is not with each other, but with the fear and bitterness that take root within. The true enemy is not a person or a party; it is the spirit of hatred that blinds us to our shared humanity.

Now, we stand in a moment of reckoning—not one of revenge, but of renewal. Each of us must decide whether we will live by truth or by convenience, by courage or by fear. I have chosen truth, though it often burns. It is through the fire of truth that we are refined and reminded of who we are meant to be.

To me, this era has always been about awakening—a reminder that no system or ideology should ever silence the human mind or spirit. Leadership, in its truest form, challenges us to think for ourselves and to rediscover the values that unite rather than divide.

The fire that began during these years continues to burn— not as a blaze of anger, but as a light of awareness. It burns in those who refuse to surrender to despair, in those who speak with conviction, and in those who believe that America's best days are not behind her, but still ahead.

I write these words not with bitterness, but with faith. Faith that truth will prevail, that courage will rise, and that we, as a people, will remember how to see each other not as enemies, but as fellow travelers seeking the same light. The fire of truth still burns—and as long as it does, hope remains.

www.ingramcontent.com/pod-product-compliance
Lightning Source LLC
Chambersburg PA
CBHW072139270326
41931CB00010B/1808